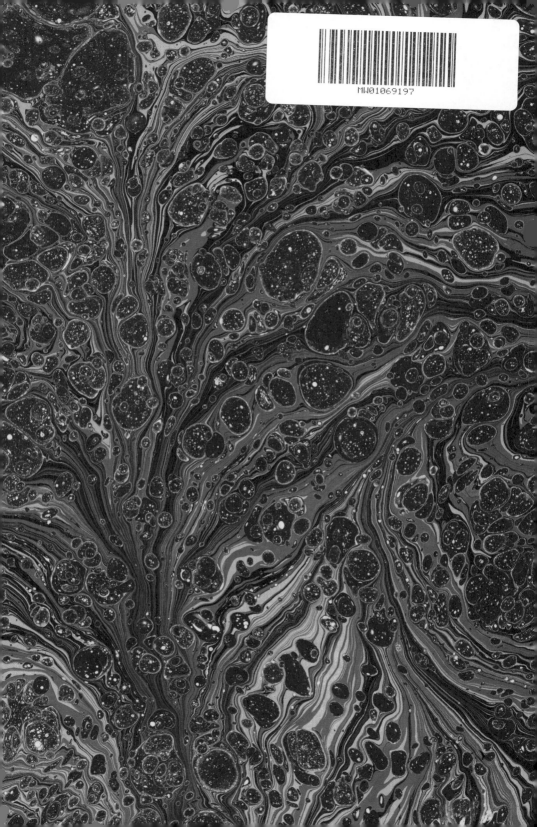

The SS-Sonderkommando "Dirlewanger": A Memoir

Edited by Rolf Michaelis

Schiffer Military History
Atglen, PA

Book translation by Omicron Language Solutions, LLC
Book design by RoS

Printed in China.
ISBN: 978-0-7643-4479-4

This book was originally published in German under the title
Erinnrungen an das SS Sonderkommando "Dirlewanger" by Michaelis-Verlag

We are interested in hearing from authors with book ideas on related topics.

Published by Schiffer Publishing Ltd.
4880 Lower Valley Road
Atglen, PA 19310
Phone: (610) 593-1777
FAX: (610) 593-2002
E-mail: Info@schifferbooks.com.

Visit our web site at: www.schifferbooks.com
Please write for a free catalog.
This book may be purchased from the publisher.
Try your bookstore first.

Table of Contents

Foreword

Ever since I began to delve into the history of the Waffen-SS in 1987 (since 1994 as a publisher), I have come in contact with around 400 former members of this troop. Numerous conversations were recorded on paper, audio tape, or video, and countless binders have been filled with recollections and documents.

With these records, I have always been able to incorporate eye-witness accounts in addition to the dry numbers and facts in the over 40 books published thus far. This not only livens things up a bit, but also puts a human face on the historical events.

Up until now, I didn't want to publish a book that was solely based on the memories of a soldier. The narrative presented here, though, is particularly interesting, because it describes the "Dirlewanger" topic from the perspective of a contemporary witness. Thus, this book functions as a supplement to previous publications: *Das SS-Sonderkommando "Dirlewanger"* and *Die SS-Sturmbrigade "Dirlewanger."* Both books, which describe the history of this special unit, were written based exclusively on documents.

In order to enable the utmost authenticity, the style has been brought into a homogeneous form. The reader can refer to the appendix for data and facts regarding the formation and deployment of the *SS-Sonderkommando* (SS Special Unit).

This book presents the recollections of a man who initially came into the so-called Wilddiebkommando Oranienburg (Oranienburg Poacher's Unit) as a poacher. After it was renamed the *SS-Sonderkommando* "Dirlewanger," deployments to Poland, Belarus, and the front followed. Not only was he a member of this special unit from its inception to the end, but he also took part in practically all of its missions. His experiences provide deep and purely subjective insights into the circumstances at that time. The narrator was, of course, shaped by this period of history, and his statements reflect the tragedies that unfolded then, and not to the degree that they would be viewed from today's perspective.

The reader should keep in mind that the operations carried out by the *SS-Sonderkommando* "Dirlewanger" brought great suffering to the Polish and Belarusian people. It would be impossible to describe this anguish here in detail. It is deplorable that the German government once ordered such atrocities! This book is presented to the public with the hope that this is never again repeated.

The man behind this story died when he was almost 86 years old. Nevertheless, it was his wish that his name remain anonymous.

BERLIN, NOVEMBER 2008
ROLF MICHAELIS

Childhood and Adolescence

I was born in 1920 in Lower Bavaria. I know nothing about my father – maybe he was the farmer who employed my mother as a maidservant, or maybe he was a farmhand. In any case, my mother had to leave her job during the pregnancy and search for a new one. This was not easy, of course, but it worked out, and she found work with another farmer. My earliest childhood memories are actually of my school days. I attended a village school beginning in 1926. There were several age groups together in one classroom, and it wasn't easy. The little ones were often bullied by the bigger kids. One time, after recess, my inkwell was missing. I didn't dare say anything. When the teacher noticed that I wrote with only a pencil, instead of with pen and ink, I admitted that I had lost my ink somewhere in the school. The teacher quickly identified the culprit. I got my inkwell back during class, and after school I got a sound beating from the rascal who had stolen it from me.

In 1934 I left school as a 14-year-old, and I was able to help out at the farm where my mother worked. Since I didn't really know how to do anything yet, the farmer usually sent me out with the foreman, who was responsible for the forest, among other things. He picked out trees that were to be harvested and sent to the sawmill, or to be used as a source of fuel for heating. The foreman was a grumpy guy who usually treated me quite harshly. He joined the SA (Sturmabteilung, Storm Detachment) and participated in his company's social evenings on weekends. He was often so drunk that someone had to pick him up from the pub and bring him back to the farm. Sometimes he would still be walking around in his SA uniform on Monday and Tuesday. He didn't take it off at all – not even at night. Because he began to drink more and more, I had a lot of time to myself and managed many tasks all alone. The farmer never caught on, and thought his foreman was doing a great job and organizing everything so well. Once, when I had to get the drunkard from the bar and bring him to his room, I noticed his rifle leaning on the wall at the head of his bed. I had never seen him with the gun, and I was quite amazed that he even had such a thing.

I spent most of my free time with my friend Gustl. We would often go out to the forest and lay snares for catching rabbits or foxes or partridges. It was all just theory, though. We never caught any wild animals. We also frequently brought along our slingshots, which we used to shoot acorns or small stones. Once in a while we would hide behind the bushes and shoot a few acorns at the ribs of old horses, just enough to make them jerk. The more they were startled, the more we chuckled. We also tried to shoot birds, but we never got one. At some point we became bored with it, which is typical with boys that age, and then I remembered the foreman's rifle. A plan was quickly hatched to take the gun out into the forest when its owner was on his weekly drinking binge at the bar. The best time was the first weekend after the foreman had received his pay. The first attempt to implement our plan failed, since during the harvest time even the foreman was needed to help out. And it was no fun to go off hunting in the woods during the winter.

The foreman, who in the meantime had risen in rank to SA-Rottenführer (Section Leader), constantly babbled about the national uprising and the liberation of Germany on our trips to fell trees. He always repeated things that he had heard somewhere – he pronounced difficult words, like plutocracy, differently every time, for example. But the Hitler Youth had not yet made its way to us. Maybe this was due to the stern faith of the rural Catholic population. In 1938, I was drafted into the RAD (Reichsarbeitsdienst, Reich Labor Service) for half a year. It was fun for me actually – big heads and country bumpkins were here together, and we all worked under the same conditions with spades, axes, and saws. One of our jobs was to build a wildlife park, with a wooden observation tower and footpaths. Early in the morning and late in the evening, I occasionally saw wild game out in the forest or grazing in the meadows, and I daydreamed about how I would bag wild boar, foxes, and deer, and hang the trophies on my wall. Then I remembered the foreman's gun again and I imagined bagging a twelve-pointer.

After being released as a laboring man, I went back to the farm. I still hadn't learned anything, and it seemed like I would probably spend the rest of my life working as a farmhand. But because I was hard-working and dependable, the future didn't look too bad. There were plenty of slackers who weren't fit to work on the farm. My monthly pay was not much, but since room and board were free, I got by okay. There wasn't a lot for me to buy – aside from cigarettes or nicer clothes.

Over the course of my intermittent daydreams as a big-game-hunter, I frequently left the farm at three a.m., met up with Gustl, and roamed through the forest. After some time we came across game trails, and stood there on the lookout. Around five am we would toddle back to begin the day's work. We thought it was pretty exciting! And then the time had come: one morning we saw deer grazing on the edge of the forest. We memorized the spot and decided to go hunting there on the weekend with the foreman's rifle.

Poaching and Prison

When the drunkard marched off to the bar around eight p.m., I entered his room and grabbed the gun – the shells were hanging in plain sight in a little bag directly behind it. Quite excited, I hid the thing under the straw mattress of my bed and hoped that it would get dark soon. Around three a.m. I climbed out of the window and met up with Gustl. We ran to the spot where we had seen the deer a few days before and hoped that the creatures would return again. And sure enough, around 3:30 am – the morning light was already announcing itself ever so slightly – they trotted out of the forest and began to pluck at the grass. We were thrilled! We had already loaded the gun and brought it into a firing position on a low-lying tree trunk. I aimed over the notch and bead sights, while Gustl told me which deer I should target. Suddenly, I felt a little uneasy about the whole thing, but the constant poking from my buddy brought me back to pulling the trigger without further contemplation!

The bang was enormous in the quiet of the morning. We were both incredibly terrified. The critters scattered – apparently I had not hit the mark. In any case, I was so scared that I wanted to get back to the farm as quickly as possible, return the gun back to its owner, and crawl back into bed unnoticed. But Gustl said, "So now we have to go over and see if you got one!" With legs shaking, we crossed the field and I hoped that we could split right away. But then there was the deer, as dead as a doornail. "Clean shot," said Gustl. But I was in no mood to celebrate! We had thought about how and where we wanted to shoot wild game, but what we would do with it afterward, we had no idea. I thought that we should take off as quickly as possible and leave the animal lying there. But Gustl said that would be a shame – we could make such nice roast venison out of it. We then decided, at my urging, to first drag the deer into the woods, cover it with brush and thick branches, and then come back the next night to haul it away.

No sooner said than done. We rushed back, said goodbye, and at around 4:30 a.m. I was back at the farm, tiptoeing to the foreman's shack. When I opened the door, two faces were looking at me. My heart stood still. Two of the boozer's SA buddies had just brought their commander back to his room – and I stood there with a gun in my hand! The guy always staggered home from the local pub at 7 a.m. or later, or even around noon the following day, and now this! They immediately asked what I was doing with the gun. I answered that I had wanted to take a look at it because I also wanted to buy one someday. They said nothing more and I left. But the disaster had already begun to run its course when Gustl and I came up with this idiotic idea to shoot wild game.

By the next day, word was already spreading that a shot had been heard in the forest. I thought to myself that if the SA men remembered me, it was all over. But that was not the case. Nevertheless I was quite shocked, and Gustl and I pondered over what we should do now with the animal in the brush. My not-so-bright pal said "Let's just leave it there. No one will find it because it's hidden." Anyway, I could hardly get any sleep. A few days later, the foreman came to me and said that his buddies had told him that I had brought his rifle back to the room. "Yeah," I sputtered, "I really wanted to take a look at the thing." Then he said: "If you were out poaching with it, there will be hell to pay. Someone was out shooting in the forest at night!" My knees suddenly got weak again.

Without consulting Gustl, I marched out at night with a shovel and wanted to bury the carcass. But try dragging a dead dear alone through the underbrush in the forest. I was in despair. I thought about just confessing everything to the farmer. Maybe it wouldn't be such a big deal. Unfortunately, a constable had already come to the farm the next day and had spoken with the farmer, who then called for me. The bloody stupid foreman had gone to the police and reported the incident with his rifle, on account of the shot in the forest. I plodded along to the farmer, who asked me in the presence of the gendarme if I had taken a shot with the foreman's rifle in the forest last week. I stood like a picture of misery in front of them, and when the gendarme, an older man, calmly said to me, "Little fellow, just confess to everything. That's the best thing you can do," I said, "Yes, it was a very dumb idea." Well, the gendarme took me to the gendarmerie station immediately. On the way there, I asked him what would happen to me. He answered that he didn't know, but without a gun license, you can neither possess a weapon nor shoot with it in the forest. I could be brought before the court already. Reality hit me like a ton of bricks! Shocked, I asked if anything could be done to reverse this so that it could simply be forgotten. "Nope," he said. "It doesn't work like that. The law is the law."

At the station he then drafted a statement, which I had to sign. But I didn't say anything about my pal Gustl. Because he said it would make things easier for me if I told the whole truth, I not only foolishly admitted that I had shot the gun, but also that I had killed a deer. That was not a good idea. But if the animal had been found, it surely would have been even worse. After the interrogation, I was allowed to go back home. What an awful feeling; I thought that everyone would know about it and would gloat over my misfortune.

First, I had to return to the farmer, who now questioned me again. But I was glad that I had already told the gendarme everything. I never needed to lie. The farmer remained relatively calm, but then he called me a poacher and said, "You're going to jail for this." With weak legs, I went to the other room to see my mother, who was waiting for me anxiously. "My boy, my boy," she cried over and over.

About a week later, I had to go to another hearing. I had really hoped and wished that nothing more would happen. A false conclusion as it turned out, of course. A plain clothes detective questioned me and wanted to hold me there. I asked, totally shocked, "You're not serious, are you? But I have to get back home to my mother and my job!"

The detective looked at me somewhat pityingly and answered that I could return home now, but I would have to bank on not going home after the trial at the district court. I was distraught.

A short time later, I had to go to court. My confession was read there in front of the gendarme and the detectives, and I was asked if everything was accurate. I affirmed, and after about an hour the verdict was given. Due to the unauthorized killing of wild game and the unlawful possession and use of a weapon, I received two years in prison! My blood ran cold and I nearly collapsed. Two years in prison only because of one silly mistake, as I saw it. But the law saw it differently. Illegal possession of a weapon and ammunition, and using it for the unlawful killing of wild game could have earned me a much harsher punishment. The judge even said that previous poachers had been hanged. I also had to compensate the farmer who owned the forest for the deer.

I couldn't believe what was happening to me, and could still barely comprehend it afterward. My mother broke down in tears, but the farmer and the foreman were obviously dissatisfied with the verdict. For me, it meant imprisonment at almost 19 years of age, beginning in the spring of 1939. It was all so unreal for me, like in a dream, and I constantly hoped to wake up. And wake up I did, every day around 5:30 a.m. in prison. First, we would wash up, and then there was breakfast. Usually there was bread with sugar beet molasses. Sometimes some cheese (curd). But apart from that, there was actually always a bland watery soup with barley or potatoes. I wasn't assigned to glue bags or to road construction. Instead, my job was to make brooms day in and day out. Pretty soon, I was sick and tired of it. Every night around 9:30 pm it was lights out. The other prisoners committed every kind of crime – from theft and receiving stolen goods to aggravated assault.

Treatment by the guards was not bad. Of course, we got no sympathy from them, but I can't say that anyone was beaten or otherwise poorly treated. We were definitely chewed out now and again, though.

Enlistment in the Wilddiebkommando Oranienburg

One day during breakfast, after a year in prison, I was ordered to see the warden. Five men were waiting there – three in plain clothes (the warden among them) and two in SS uniforms (one in black and the other in gray), one of whom was thumbing through my files. The two men in uniform looked me up and down, whispered with one another, and then talked quietly with the three plainclothes men. Then the warden said to me: "You were sentenced to two years in prison for poaching and still have one year to serve. You have the opportunity to be released now if you voluntarily register for military service. The Führer has enacted an order that allows poachers who have killed wild game with a gun to be rehabilitated." He looked at the other men quizzically. The one who held my file in his hands asked me, "So you took down a buck with your first shot? And you never fired a gun before that? Did you ever do anything wrong before that?" I answered with yes and no, and then the man smiled and said, "He's our guy. We'll take him."

Then another plainclothes man spoke to me – I assume he was from the criminal investigation department or the public prosecutor's office. He told me that if I registered, then my remaining sentence would be remitted and I would become a respectable member of society again.

The Polish campaign had victoriously come to an end within a month. Norway and Denmark had just been occupied, and German mountain troops, paratroopers, and sailors were fighting in Narvik against the English. We had been at war with France for over half a year now without a large-scale escalation of combat operations – the French called it "Dröle de Guerre" – but it was clear that this would change under the right conditions. I wanted be there and teach those cheeky frogs (as we called them then) a lesson. I gave my consent.

"Great," the gentlemen said, and I was free to go. Shortly after, the French campaign began and I was still sitting in the factory hall making brooms. At the end of June 1940, France capitulated, and I was called in to make myself ready to travel the following day. I wasn't told where I was going. The next morning, a plainclothes man – from the criminal investigation department I assumed – picked me up. We drove to the train station and took a train from there to Oranienburg, with train changes in Nuremberg and Berlin. From the Oranienburg station we walked about 15 minutes to the Sachsenhausen concentration camp. The detective handed my papers over to the guard and disappeared.

There was a telephone call, and about ten minutes later an SS-man came to get me. We went to a barracks called a barracks block, where several plainclothes men were standing. Their appearances and ages were completely different. Short and fat, tall and skinny, old and young – all were represented. At some point, an SS-man stepped out of the barracks and said that we would now undergo a medical examination to find out if we were fit. We had to undress and then march in a duck gait to a room where several tables were lined up. We were weighed and measured, we answered questions, and we also had to read off letters from a plaque on the wall. In addition to one civilian, there were several SS-men and SS-officers present – some wearing a doctor's white coat. In total, it lasted about two hours for us all. Then, an SS-man led us to another wooden barracks. He said that we were not permitted to leave the barracks without his permission, and then he disappeared into a small, separate room.

We sat on stools in the room, and some sat on their beds. At first there wasn't much talking. Just the usual "Where are you from? What were you hired for? How did it go for you?" It appeared that practically all of us were from the south of the German Reich; a few were from Ostmark or Sudetenland. I think maybe four or five came from East Prussia. Meanwhile, it was already evening, and the *Unterscharführer* (Junior Squad Leader) led us to dinner. After having the same meal practically every day in prison, I was delighted with the variety here: there was sliced bread and liverwurst.

The next day, at 4:45 a.m., we were awakened by the *Unterscharführer*, "*Wilddiebkommando*, rise and shine!" So now we knew what we were called – we were the *Wilddiebkommando*. There was a washroom in the middle of the barracks where we could quickly make our morning toilet run. After that, four men were sent off to get breakfast, which we had in the barracks. There was coffee, bread, and milk soup. It wasn't much better than prison food, though.

The first exercises began in civilian clothes – lining up and marching in formation. For lunch we got tea, fish, and potato soup, and then about an hour of rest in the barracks. Then we lined up in front of the barracks. Around four to five men had to step forward; they grabbed their stuff from the barracks and then they were led away. Apparently they had failed the physical from the previous day. In total we now numbered around 90 men, and the exercises continued. For dinner there was tea (again), bread, and some kind of jellied meat. This routine was repeated for another two days, until we all received old drill uniforms. We had to lay our civilian clothes in cardboard boxes and write our addresses on them. Everything was then brought to the office to be mailed home. Now, we had discernibly become soldiers.

We saw the actual prisoners of the concentration camp, too. In the mornings, they lined up there. If I remember correctly, they also lined up at midday, and of course there were the evening roll calls. They always wore their white and blue-striped prison clothes with the appropriate inverted triangle to indicate why they were imprisoned. I also remember the boot walkers – prisoners who made up a special squad that had to break in jackboots all day long so the soldiers on the front wouldn't get excessive blistering on their feet from new boots. We often heard the prisoners singing, too,

Dr. Oskar Dirlewanger

while they marched back and forth over the grounds. We did the same thing, but we had to learn other songs. We had no contact with them, so I couldn't find out anything more about the prisoners at that time.

The mood among the men wasn't bad. We were happy to have made it out of the penal system, and some even wanted to participate on the front. Others, though, were lone wolves, or made a wholly unpleasant or untrustworthy impression. On around the third day, Dirlewanger came to us and introduced himself as our superior. We lined up in the morning, as we always did, when he approached us – I think he was the rank of *Hauptsturmführer* (Chief Assault Leader) then – accompanied by some other SS-men. He was an unbelievably scrawny and tall figure with a wrinkled face. I think he was almost 6 feet 3 inches. He addressed us in a Swabian dialect, which doesn't exactly sound so tough, and it went something like, "You are all poachers, and the Führer has decided to give you a chance to prove yourselves. Take this opportunity seriously and show that you are real men! If you don't, you will end up where you started."

Dirlewanger didn't seem very likeable, but my old foreman, who had stabbed me in the back at the gendarmerie station, would have been even less likeable. The SS-men who had come along took over all functions as squad leader, platoon leader, etc. A first sergeant was there, and managed the orderly room where we received our pay books the next day. Now we were all suddenly members of the SS. Within the next few days we were led to the garment barracks, and the clothing supervisor gave each of us a field blouse, pants, cap, helmet, and everything else one would get as a new soldier of the Führer – everything from handkerchiefs to shoe brushes.

We had to put all of our stuff neatly away in a little locker in our barracks, but we weren't allowed to lock it. The next morning, already in proper field dress, the real training began. In addition to the drill exercises, saluting lessons followed – always three steps away in front of a superior, with a raised right hand. This was followed by weapons training and our first target practice on the shooting range. A first shot was fired at the test target, and then any deviation was shown to the shooter so that he knew how he should aim his piece in order to hit the target. On top of that, shooting theory was also taught.

In the evening, after cleaning the rifles (all of them Karabiner 98k), they were delivered to the armory. Marching songs were then rehearsed, and we went to eat in the food barracks of the SS guard battalion. Curfew was 10 pm.

Deployment to the General Government

After about two months we were renamed the *SS-Sonderkommando* "Dirlewanger" and relocated to the General Government. In the Lublin district, we were supplied with living quarters by Globocnik, the SS and police leader there. In addition to further training, we also took part in several operations. This usually included searching homes and businesses for Jews and Poles. But generally, we were only there to act as a barricade while the police carried out the actual searches and arrests.

In the fall of 1940, we left Lublin by train and were relocated near the Ukrainian border in the area between Jaroslaw and Tomaszow. We were placed under the command of a police battalion there, and assigned with guarding a small camp of Jews in Dzikow-Stary, among other things. The entire population of Jewish men from the surrounding areas was detained there – about 200 of them, who were mainly tasked with road construction. It was a terrible thing for those who had never done anything like it before and were not in the physical condition required for that kind of work. They stood around with sweat-covered faces and sticky hair on their midday break, looking at us angrily. While it was embarrassing for me, I heard others say things like, "Don't look so cockeyed, you dumb Jewish pig, or I'll pop you in the mouth!" But there were also those among us who said, "Whoa now, come on, relax. These guys are just poor bastards, and six months ago you were sitting in jail, too." But it could also get nasty when the hotheads were by themselves. They would kick them in the ass and slap them, or hit them with a branch or the butt of their rifle.

Unfortunately, the large distances away from superior authorities spawned a tendency for many to take matters into their own hands. We were often used for raids, and had to screen civilians or search homes. It quickly became common practice to steal things. Sometimes it was a clock or silverware – the moral borders soon disappeared almost completely – sometimes you took rings off or demanded money and jewelry.

Someone must have started it, and then almost all of us were doing it, I have to say. Some became more and more impudent and blackmailed Jews and Poles. "If you don't give me this and this tomorrow, you'll end up in a prison camp." That was going too far for me. We didn't have the brightest guys in our *Sonderkommando*, and this became public. In addition to complaints by the Poles, and even partly by the Jews, to other Germans in uniform, the jewelry dealings eventually got the attention of some higher-up German authorities. No one really cared if you had three or four rings and

The *SS-Sonderkommando* "Dirlewanger" encountered many Jewish people in Poland.

other valuables and then started to sell or swap the stuff. But when a few idiots offered jewelry or silver to some members of the *Wehrmacht*, they were, of course, surprised, and wondered where we were getting so many valuables. Like I said, the word got out quickly.

Back then our *Sonderkommando* was made up of about 100 men, and we had only two or three officers. One of them was Dirlewanger, whom we rarely saw. I don't think that he took part in this kind of petty crime, but I can imagine that he blackmailed the Jews, and did so on a larger scale than we did. Anyway, beginning in the summer of 1941, several investigators from the SS and Police Court in Krakow came and interrogated us. Interestingly enough, we were also asked if we knew whether Dirlewanger had had a liaison with a Jewish woman. I didn't notice anything, at least not in Poland. Later on, in Belarus, I did see it. Dirlewanger had a weakness for slim women, and these were usually Jewish women – the natives were often on the bigger side. Anyway, he was said to have had an intimate relationship with a Jewish woman who worked as an interpreter. After the war, I learned from a magazine that Dirlewanger had already sat in jail before the war for seducing an underage girl.

The detectives' questioning also touched on the jewelry, money, etc., which was illegally taken from the Poles and Jews and put up for sale – in all actuality, it involved theft and receiving of stolen goods. There were a lot of dimwits in our group, and that's why it became a big deal. They ran their mouths, or naively said things like, "We got the stuff from the Jews." Even Dirlewanger was visibly uneasy when you saw him. We were all really nervous too, actually, until some really slick guys said, "You have to prove it was me first."

Anyway, the activities of the SS and Police Court in Krakow ensured that we were brought back to reality again and no longer behaved like bulls in a china shop. Nevertheless, some remained restless, because even though the wheels of justice were grinding slowly, something had been set in motion and its conclusion was not yet certain. And with probation and a return to a normal life, things were now even more uncertain! At the end of 1941, we found out that the entire *Sonderkommando* would be relocated to Russia.

Whether that was supposed to represent a punishment or was somehow initiated by Dirlewanger, who had certain contacts in the SS leadership, I don't know. Considering the head-in-the-sand politics, it was, at least for me, good to get away from the area and the grip of the SS and Police Court in Krakow. I thought someone would have to set fire to the court so that all the files would burn. That was my mindset as a 21-year-old.

Relocation to Belarus

At the end of January 1942, we (by then around 160 men) relocated to Belarus. We traveled via Kowel and Korosten to Mogilev in an E-transport. We relieved a police company there and were housed in a two-story building that used to be an old-age home. There wasn't much furniture, and it had to be requested. Dirlewanger was really worked up about it and called it a huge mess. The bosses would sleep in white beds, and we didn't even have straw mattresses. So we organized some straw, and about three days later a truck came with beds and lockers, which we unloaded and carried to our rooms. With hovering around minus 25° C most nights, it was everything but pleasant. There was central heating in the basement that we started and heated with anything that would burn. Fortunately, the boiler, water pipes, and radiators were all working, so that we could at least warm up the building a bit.

The mood of the group was more relaxed here than it was in Poland. For starters, we weren't subjected to criminal prosecution. Otherwise, it was worlds apart from Poland. Sure, everything was quite primitive in the area where we were deployed, but somehow you felt closer to home. Because the area had previously belonged to the Imperial and Royal Monarchy, it resembled Germany more than Belarus in some way. Mogilev was heavily damaged, and in the winter every city is pretty desolate anyway. There were a lot of uniformed soldiers and few civilians. Civilians were usually all headed to the same place, a kind of marketplace where they sold everything that they could spare: from frozen potatoes and apples to single shoes or torn jackets and pants.

Basically, all of the people there were poor. But I didn't get the impression that it really bothered them that much. The Russians have always had it rough. Under the Tsar, the average citizen had nothing; under Stalin, it was probably no different. Because the people there all had nothing, we were also no longer tempted to take something away from them. We didn't get a lot of supplies, and so the winter was quite dismal in Mogilev. We were under the command of Von dem Bach, the Higher SS and Police leader for central Russia. I saw him a few times, and found him to be quite a conceited guy who enjoyed his role as the master of life and death of the civilian population, as well as his own underlings. Dirlewanger was a different kind of commander, but more on that later. We were used primarily in the area of the Jewish ghetto in Mogilev. Our job included patrols and raids, among other things. It was hard to believe the valuables the Jews would hide, even in this situation. I honestly believe that jewelry and any objects of art (even paintings) were often more important to them than getting something to eat!

The houses in the ghetto didn't have any electricity, and were therefore always very dark. The windows were often covered or nailed shut, since the glass had been broken out. Inside, candles or tallow lights burned. Eight, ten, or twenty people would be situated there in a very confined space. We went into these rooms with flashlights, pulled the curtains back or broke the wood away from the windows with our gun butts, and then saw the frightened faces. Due to missing sanitary facilities, there was often a dreadful stink in the rooms. We later encountered the same thing in the Russian villages. Apparently, hygiene or simple washing was not so commonplace. During the searches shots were also fired. I remember how a member of our commando repeatedly shot at people during the operations.

Dirlewanger's sex drive kicked in again somehow, and he began to provide accommodations for some nice looking Jewish girls. They cleaned the office and rooms for Dirlewanger and the junior officers. They received proper boarding – and the men most likely had intimate relations with them, too. The Higher SS and Police Leader was probably informed beforehand of the incidents in Poland, and so he had kept a close eye on our *Sonderkommando*. In any case, members of the SD came by several times and eventually demanded the surrender of the Jewish girls. Dirlewanger told them that they worked for the *Sonderkommando* and would not hand them over. He didn't care. I assume that he was then asked by the chief of the *SS-Hauptamt* (SS Head Office), Berger, to straighten out, because shortly afterward the girls were gone. Whether they went back to the ghetto or not, I don't know. After the war, I was also asked by criminal investigators about it. There was an accusation that Dirlewanger had the girls shot. But I don't believe it because that wasn't his style. Anyway, we noticed that we were under observation, and that was surely the reason for many not to behave at their own discretion. But that changed again later when we were relocated off the beaten track in a small village and had no one controlling us from above.

In addition to the assignments in Mogilev we were also utilized for intelligence purposes in the forests surrounding Mogilev in the spring of 1942. Together with police units, we were supposed to find out where partisans had stayed, where they were now, and what kind of numbers they had. Due to the weather conditions, we could only push forward into the forested regions with sleds. These sleds were pulled by panja horses (small Russian steppe horses that had really shaggy coats and received little care from the locals, but were unbelievably tame and efficient). The results of our reconnaissance missions were modest. The partisans went out of the way of such scheduled actions, and in order to take a more active role, we would have to be more mobile. We also didn't have the right clothing at all for these hard winters, with temperatures reaching minus 40° C. We wore our shirts with a pullover and a field blouse over it, then our thin summer coats and a camouflage jacket. In addition to our long underwear, which we always wore (even in the summer!), we only had cloth trousers and our jackboots. To protect ourselves a bit from the freezing cold, we stuffed crumpled newspaper in our clothes, but it didn't help much. If the operation lasted more than one day, we would stay in a village when possible. This, of course, gave us the advantage of having a roof over our heads, but also meant that the operation was no longer as flexible. Also, you would always come into contact with lice in Russian huts.

When it became milder in April, more active partisan fighting began. Initially, they carried out attacks primarily on supply lines. That meant railway lines were blown up and supply convoys ambushed. To defend these attacks, posts and support points were set up on these supply lines. These were usually fortified wooden bunkers or less developed villages, which were also attacked – usually at night. We were also sent to these support points on various occasions. I once sat with four fellow soldiers in a wooden bunker that was lined with wooden palisades and observed what took place on the track in front of us and in the area around us.

During the daytime it was not so exciting. Normally, only German trucks drove by. If a Russian came by, we would go out and check his papers, which would normally state that Ivan was a resident of so and so village, and that he had permission to go here and there. Sometimes the papers were not in order and we would have to arrest the Russian. We usually handed him over to passing soldiers, who turned him in at a post in the next town.

The mentality of the Russians was like this: some got worked up and gabbled about, and wouldn't calm down until someone smacked them. Others just stood there, silent and lethargic, and all you could do was shake your head. Then we would say, "Okay, Ivan. Come with me and wait here!" (Idi suda Iwan, padashdi sdjessj!). At night it was all a lot less pleasant. You always had to be prepared to be fired at or attacked in some way. And you couldn't see anything. While the others slept in the wooden bunker, making various sounds, one would always stand guard for about two hours. If you heard a noise, it was almost always partisans. The villagers were not allowed to leave their village after 9 p.m. at the latest. Normally, you didn't hear anything, since the partisans, of course, knew where all posts and support points were and avoided them. But when you did hear something, you knew immediately that something was in the bushes.

In 1942, however, the partisans were actually still relatively cautious, and were more likely to attack supply lines or telephone poles than military units. One of our few trucks, an Opel Blitz, was once ambushed, though. The driver and the other soldiers on board were killed. A Russian reported the incident, and eventually we were alerted and had to go there as quickly as possible. The partisans had already disappeared, of course. I don't remember anymore whether they had plundered the bodies. In any case, the fallen were not maimed; I saw this later on sometimes, and it was a horrible sight!

In the summer of 1942, we were continually sent on reconnaissance patrols from Mogilev to the surrounding forests and marshland areas. We were always on the lookout for civilians who were prowling around somewhere in the forest. They weren't allowed to be out there. If you saw someone there, you could be sure that it was a partisan. As soon as you made eye contact, they would usually make themselves scarce. We, of course, shot after them, but rarely hit the target. Then the area would be searched, and once in a while we found partisan camps. Sometimes these were

Fortified support point in Belarus.

burrows, sometimes real log houses. While some of us stood guard, others searched these shelters. Occasionally, you would find food or clothing – the partisans didn't have much either. Then the camps were always burned or bombed with hand grenades.

In the summer of 1942, the *SS-Sonderkommando* took part in larger combat operations against the partisans, with Mogilev as the base. Around 6,000 or more men from different German security divisions and the Higher SS and Police Leader were deployed. First, they encircled a wide area, and then worked their way to the middle, sometimes in two-week operations. Since the area was full of thick forest and marshes, we managed to hatch out the partisans through the existing gaps in the first few days. Actually, you could almost call it drive hunting. It's interesting that the partisans always retreated. With the exception of a few smaller shoot outs, they hardly ever lined up against us openly. They usually dragged all of their belongings in front of us until they couldn't anymore, and then they surrendered to the inevitable skirmish. They were usually leftovers from the original partisans in the area. Many of them attempted adventurous escapes. Probably only in exceptional cases, but they tried this, too: the partisans would jump in water holes and pools and breathe through hollow reeds. When we searched the civilians we normally didn't find any weapons. I think that the partisans, at least at that point in time, probably had big supply difficulties. Sometimes they also threw their stuff in the water, or hid it somewhere and masqueraded as simple civilians. Some even had valid papers on hand, but they only applied to other areas. This actually only showed that those who had valid papers could also be partisans.

The partisans that we got a hold of, and their families (the partisans often lived with their wives and children in the forest or in the marshes), were frequently shot on the spot. The same also applied if someone was shot at from a village or its vicinity. In this case, we were again alerted and moved into the village as quickly as possible. The village was cordoned off to prevent the escape of the residents, and all of the cottages were searched and vacated. This happened so often that you just walked in and screamed, "Dawaj, dawaj. Get out of here!" Then the house was searched for anything suspicious: a weapon, a uniform, or any kind of flyer. The Russians didn't have much, and hardly anything apart from food found its way into the haversack. If residents resisted verbally or with violence, they were shot immediately inside the house. In these cases, legitimation was of no interest whatsoever.

The others were rounded up, and either shot down with a machine gun or locked in a magazine (often a former church), which was then set ablaze. A couple of hand grenades were thrown in, and then we waited to see how the fire developed.

That was all part of safeguarding the hinterlands then. They were nothing more than enemies to us. We were shot at and reacted to it. To ensure that we were never shot at by the same people, we liquidated them. These were the orders we received. That can't be, and shouldn't be, an excuse, but only an explanation. We were deliberately trained not to think in the Third Reich. "Obedient 'til death," the maxim goes. But only those who experienced it themselves can comprehend it. Today, people are much more self-aware in the way they think and act than previous generations.

(TOP) THE GHETTO IN MOGILEV.

(MIDDLE) HANGED PARTISANS AND PARTISAN SYMPATHIZERS.

(BOTTOM) LAHOYSK.

Villages that harbored partisans were generally burned to the ground.

After larger operations, previous pockets were combed through again for weapons, devices, and any remaining partisans. During such operations, or simple reconnaissance missions, we encountered partisans from time to time, even quite suddenly. This usually resulted in an immediate exchange of gunfire. Because the Karabiner was not suitable for abrupt, short-range battles, we tried to acquire Soviet sub-machine guns. The ammunition was relatively easy to find in the camps of partisans; there were always a lot of things buried on the periphery.

Still in 1942, we received the order that villages not be burnt to the ground anymore. We didn't entirely understand, since that had been the standard directive since the spring. We didn't question it for long. The so-called gang of suspects was no longer to be shot, but rather brought to prison camps. We wondered and asked ourselves if workers were needed. And a few weeks later, the actual request followed: every captive partisan was also able to work in the German armament industry. Aha, we thought, the orders had actually changed a great deal. Before this we had roamed the area trying to kill partisans. And now we were deployed to collect as many work-capable partisans as possible, and to prey on the inventory of the living and the dead. In other words, round up cattle and agricultural products. By restricting recruiting and reinforcement possibilities, we deprived the partisans of their existence.

Dirlewanger frequently took reconnaissance flights with a Fieseler-Storch aircraft from the Higher SS and Police Leader. From up above, he could see the trails through the forests and marshes, as well as the camps and positions of the partisans. This, of course, helped a lot. In the meantime, the partisans had found a new strategy, and laid mines everywhere possible. They built thousands of small wooden mines in their own woodworking shops. Unlike German land mines, with metal housing, these mines could not be located by the mine detectors of the pioneers. Some of us were even killed by them. One time, an Opel Blitz drove over a mine and both of the driver's feet were blown off. Dirlewanger, who was a very pragmatic thinker, simply made the suspected partisan population march in front of us after that. This frequently led to gruesome scenes, and I will never forget the dull explosions of the mines. Normally, the people were dead on the spot or seriously injured – it affected me to experience that up close, but of course, it was preferable to having stepped on the mine yourself.

After bringing Ukrainians and Russians in from time to time, starting in the spring of 1942, the *SS-Sonderkommando* achieved battalion strength for the first time with the addition of two companies made up of Russian volunteers. The Ukrainians, who we had first, were nicer. They were recruited in prisoner of war camps, and they were all tall and blond. They probably all came from western Ukraine, and some even spoke in broken German. I found the Russians to be unpleasant. Apart from a few exceptions, they were sly journeymen, and all quite addicted to alcohol. We, of course, had this problem in our ranks as well, but with the Russians it was completely out of control. Back then, no one made a big deal about it. Looking back, though, I would say that most were happy to have authority over others – over their fellow countrymen, of course. They ran around with clubs, reeking of sweat and feces, and clobbered people when they felt like it. They obeyed us Germans, though.

"Gypsies" and "Old Fighters" Strengthen the SS-Sonderbataillon "Dirlewanger"

As part of setting up the *SS-Sonderbataillon* "Dirlewanger" in late-summer 1942, we also received reinforcements from Germany. Among them, actually, were German gypsies who had been imprisoned in the Oranienburg concentration camp! They arrived with shaved heads, and it was really hard to believe that they were walking around in SS uniforms – without collar patches, though.

We didn't have a collar patch in the beginning, either, but later we got the normal ones with SS runes. And in early 1943, a collar patch with two crossed rifles with a stick hand grenade underneath was stitched on. Gypsies running around in SS uniforms now was just as paradoxical as it was when we were hanging around in SS uniforms as ex-prisoners. Although some of us were rehabilitated as early as 1943, and some even later, we had already obtained ranks. By the end of 1942 I was, together with some others, appointed to *SS-Sturmmann* (Storm Trooper) by Dirlewanger. Naturally, we celebrated. A special organizer brought us a pair of roasted chickens – there were pigs running around too, but they were more difficult to nab during operations, and we were also afraid of trichinae, although this was more common in wild pigs. Plenty of alcohol was consumed, and at 22 years of age, I was now an *SS-Sturmmann*, after having previously been a convicted poacher. My rehabilitation followed in 1943. The jackass from the orderly room came to me and said, "I wrote your rehabilitation today. Congratulations!" I was delighted, although it was only a recommendation from Dirlewanger, and it still had to be decided in Germany. I wasn't actually rehabilitated until 1944.

In 1942, some very strange men on probation came to us a few times. They were veteran party members, so-called old fighters, who I assume belonged to the general SS, but served in the *Wehrmacht* or the NSKK, or somewhere, and had done something wrong. Then they came to Dirlewanger on probation. They looked like they had served their time at headquarters. They mainly just told stories about how things were elsewhere or at home, and then went off on a patrol or on some other small, mostly risk-free mission. Afterward, Dirlewanger wrote a report about how brave the party members had conducted themselves in a heavy partisan battle, and the men returned. I wondered if I would have gone to prison if had been a party member back then.

While women and children were enlisted for work assignments, hundreds of thousands of men volunteered for German military service. The *SS-Sonderbataillon* "Dirlewanger" temporarily consisted of three so-called "Russian" companies.

Awarding the Ostvolk Medal.

The Partisan War, 1943

In contrast to the winter of 1941/42, numerous larger operations were carried out against the partisans in the winter of 1942/43. This was due to the fact that the partisans had become incredibly strong, and we couldn't take the liberty of being on the defensive for six months. On the other hand, the German equipment (padded winter clothing, for example) had become better. Also, we had learned a lot in the last few months and from our first Russian winter. Our mobility was enhanced considerably with horses and sleds, and inserting so-called foreign troops on the German side also improved our capabilities, because they were at least familiar with the climate and the geographic conditions.

During these operations, fierce battles were now happening more frequently. The partisans had obtained heavy weaponry, which had been airdropped. Among their heavy artillery was the multipurpose 76mm divisional gun, which we called the "rip-boom" because impact came so fast after firing. The partisans had also set up legitimate positions, which we really had to storm, just like on the front lines. Everything was more organized than in early 1942. Back then, the partisans had to wait and see how they would get their weapons and equipment. They could pick up part of it from the remains of encirclement battles in the forests and marshes, and part of it also came from attacks on German soldiers. There were even cases where female partisans engaged with privates to get weapons in return for services, or they would distract them while others stole things. One time we also received a visit from SD. He had somehow received information that a Jew named Grynszpan was trying to hawk weapons off on the partisans at exorbitant prices. We were to search for him during reconnaissance operations. But aside from some unclear information from various civilians and stupid gossip from drunken security service members (Russians, who were engaged as auxiliary policemen in the villages), nothing ever came of it.

From 1943 on, the partisans were serious opponents. While our equipment was frequently improvised, the other side obtained superb equipment in ever-increasing amounts, including armored vehicles and even entire radio installations. Eventually, it went so far that we were continually replaced by police tanks during large operations. They were useful for battles in towns, or over open spaces at least. In the forest they were not as reliable.

Even though new policies had been introduced at the end of 1942, particularly difficult operations took place again in the spring of 1943. I almost think that it was

CRUELTY IN A WAR BEHIND THE FRONT LINES.

due to the defeat in Stalingrad – we wanted to prove that we weren't beaten and organized intense operations. Entire areas were to be depopulated, and that meant shooting everyone. Most villages consisted of maybe fifteen houses, and many people were no longer there – the men who were fit for military service were with the Red Army or the partisans – so only women and children, the elderly, and the sick were on site.

We received the order to annihilate all villages in this and that area. Because this occurred without any previous clashes with partisans, some of us had our qualms. If someone had been shot at and this was some kind of revenge expedition, then it was different. But simply driving into a village and shooting people in their homes or standing outside was bad. The recently recruited gypsies, in particular, were shocked. Dirlewanger had no respect for them anyway, and I think at least one of them was shot for some reason or another. A few others, who didn't want to participate, were sent back to Germany and returned to the Oranienburg concentration camp, or the prison they were in previously.

Operation in the Minsk Ghetto

In April 1943, there was a big operation in Minsk with a total of around 6,000 men, mainly police units. We were brought by truck from our new accommodations in Lahoysk to Minsk, about 25 km away, and we were instructed to guard the ghetto there. While the police combed through every part of the city and picked up those who didn't have valid papers (for work assignments in the Reich), we bolstered surveillance of the ghetto. The ghetto around the Jewish cemetery was fenced in with barbed wire and surrounded by several watchtowers. There were over 5,000 Jews living in the ghetto under exceptionally bad conditions. Without sufficient hygiene and food, the people – many of whom spoke German, amazingly – left a horrible impression. The houses in which they lived were all in ruins. No windows, completely ramshackle, filthy and full of vermin. It was quite strange hearing German spoken there, and we had a lot of contact, because we had to lead the work gangs to their work places at Telefunken or the National Railway. At least I saw a different side of the Jews here, compared to those in Poland or Russia. But I think it was the same for most of us – as soon as we heard German, we were a bit more tolerant. We also had to search the people to see if they were trying to smuggle something into the ghetto. With the Russian Jews this was done rather brutally; with the Germans, we asked if they had anything on them and lightly frisked their coats and jackets on the surface. It still seems strange to me today: while we found the Russian Jews repulsive, we felt sorry for the German Jews. But everyone had their own ideas.

In any case, I had my qualms about these operations against proper civilians, those who didn't act against us in any way. I would rather have gone to the forests hunting partisans or fought directly against the Red Army. This here, it wasn't my thing.

After almost a week, we went back to Lahoysk. The police had collected enough people without valid papers. Two days later we left Lahoysk again, and were supposed to secure workers, livestock, and food. With the impressions of how the German Jews in the Minsk ghetto were treated, I viewed the following operation with different eyes. We went to the scheduled area by truck and requisitioned panje wagons there, which were then driven by Russians in our commando. Everything was reloaded, and with the exception of our motorcycle squadron and our own trucks, we continued on by foot. As we drew near, life in the small villages went on as usual. Those who had the jitters or belonged to the partisans tried to hide or disappear. And they were good at it.

(TOP) THE JEWISH GHETTO IN MINSK.
(BOTTOM) THE OFFICE OF THE BELARUS KOMMISSAR GENERAL IN MINSK.

Decorations and Leave

Early in 1943, I was awarded the Infantry Assault Badge, as well as the Iron Cross, 2nd Class for the campaigns against the partisans, during which we had stormed a few enemy camps. I was quite proud of myself, and in 1943 I also got my first leave. First, I went by truck from Lahoysk to Minsk, and from there by train over Brest-Litovsk into the General Government, and then over Wartheland to Berlin and home. When I went to see my mother, there was a lot of excitement at the farm. I of course went to see the farmer too, and saw him first to ask where my mother was. His eyes grew big in amazement – there I was in an SS uniform with an Iron Cross, the Infantry Assault Badge, and a stripe on my left shoulder which identified me as a Storm Trooper. The farmer was speechless when he saw me. He had already learned from my mother that I had voluntarily signed up for the military, but he couldn't believe it, and only asked me where I was stationed and how the mood on the front lines was. I told him that I was engaged in combat against partisans in Russia – actually, it was Belarus. But for us, everything east of the General Government was Russia. The farmer didn't know what to say, because he had no idea what partisans were. Well anyway, I was allowed into the kitchen and we were given something to eat. With that he said goodbye and was visibly happy about it. That evening I met with my mother, who was overjoyed and immediately cried. I didn't know what to say. In 1943, so many had already been killed in action – even some from our village. Unfortunately, my pal Gustl, who was with me when I shot the buck, was one of them. It was all kind of strange. I went to prison and lived; he was free and was killed in Crimea in 1942. Russia was a bone mill and a giant coffin for Germany. I, of course, had to tell where I was stationed and if it was dangerous. I comforted her, and said that I was behind the front lines looking for armed civilians. She was a bit reassured. I had to register at the local authority, and then I got food stamps, all of which I gave to my mother. She always brought me food from the kitchen, even though it wasn't really allowed. The farmer probably guessed, but didn't want to say anything. He either felt a sting of remorse, since I went to prison because of him, or he was afraid that I could do something to hurt him.

I also saw the drunkard foreman a few times. At first he didn't recognize me at all and didn't speak a word to me. My mother asked me what I wanted to do after the war, and if I wanted to work here again; maybe I should talk to the farmer about it already. I didn't really get a lot of information about the war situation. There was news about Stalingrad and Tunis, but how it looked otherwise, even the generals themselves probably knew very little. We only knew about our little operational area, and a victory over the partisans was not in the foreseeable future. On the contrary, they were becoming more and more organized and stronger. I assumed that even after a final victory, we ourselves could not be discharged because all of the occupied areas would have to be secured. But I hoped that I could somehow go to France. There, according to the stories from others who had been stationed there, everything was different – similar to home, actually. Not this filth and danger of being shot from behind or stepping on a mine.

Back to Belarus with Career Criminals

Just before the end of my leave, I received a telegram requesting me to report to the commander of the *Sachsenhausen* concentration camp in Oranienburg on Monday, June 14, 1943. I was shocked! Did this have something to do with the proceedings in the General Government? Was my parole denied? Did I have to go back to prison? This made the last few days at home really stressful for me. My mother noticed and asked what was wrong. I explained my fears to her, and she was completely terrified. "My God, My God," she babbled on and on. I took the train to Berlin and then took the city train to Oranienburg. Little had changed there. I still knew the way from the train station to the concentration camp and went by foot. I asked for the commander and showed the telegram. At first, no one in the office knew anything, and they asked me to wait. Then someone came and asked me if I belonged to the *Sonderkommando* "Dirlewanger." I said yes, and I was sent back to the camp gate in a flash. I showed the slip of paper, and then I was to report to the barracks. Some other soldiers who had also been summoned here from leave arrived, as well as some members from the guard detail of the concentration camp. In all, we were about 25 men. A *Hauptsturmführer* came and explained to us that we were to take prisoners to Russia with us. This was a relief for me. I had my doubts. There were around 340 prisoners, most of whom were career criminals serving time in the concentration camp. Quite a few of them had been prisoner functionaries, mostly *kapos*. The next day they lined up. Just a week earlier they had their say over the other prisoners, and now suddenly they were left carrying the can. In retrospect, I can hardly imagine that they had all volunteered. Here in the concentration camp, they had a comfortable life as *kapos*. They had their boys who did everything for them; they could do their business while you were outside in combat freezing your ass off.

They stood there now, lined up in front of us, and I thought to myself, I wouldn't want to meet any of these guys in a dark alley. These were generally people who had made their living through crime – they hadn't made just a one-time mistake, like I did with the stupid deer. Still, I had a stripe on my sleeve, an Iron Cross in my buttonhole, and the Infantry Assault Badge on the left breast pocket of my field blouse. At least I stood out with that. The prisoners all wore plain clothes, and I would say they ranged in age from mid-20s to mid-40s. The days before moving out to Belarus were filled with exercises. Squads, platoons, and companies were formed, and marching and muster were practiced. They already knew this from the concentration camp – they had been in charge there, but here they had to obey. Each of them was issued a pay book, and they were now members of the *Waffen-SS*. What a paradox! After around two weeks, we left *Sachsenhausen* and marched to the train station, where we took a train to Berlin. We traveled through the General Government via Brest-Litovsk and Petrikovo to Bobruysk. In the southwestern part of the city there was a work camp for Jews that worked in connection with an SS troop supply camp. Our prisoners got their clothes here. They received mended SS uniforms from the workshops and the mood changed immediately. Now they felt like someone again, and they immediately considered the Russians as well as the Jewish workers to be underprivileged *muschiks* and *muselmann* inmates.

In a liberated mood, we continued on to Lahoysk via Minsk. Arriving there, the approximately 340 men formed two companies, which, for the time being, functioned as so-called recruit companies. Unlike most of us former poachers, these men had never fired a gun before and only knew a few of the orders from roll calls in the concentration camps. So, we taught them the military orders and commands here. Most of the men weren't very motivated. In the concentration camp they didn't have to do anything but push the other prisoners to work, which included a lot of harassment. Here they were all equals now and had no desire for duty; they only wanted to lead a lax existence. Discipline was not the best. Shortly after arrival in Lahoysk, Dirlewanger had both companies line up and addressed them, saying:

> The Führer has given you the opportunity to become respectable members of the national community again. He released you from the concentration camp and made you available for service here. Those who conduct themselves bravely and cleanly can have their sentences remitted. Those who act like dogs, as they did in the past, will immediately return to where they came from! Do you understand?

We officers stood near, and afterward were briefed on our new official positions by the Battalion Sergeant. For me, it meant taking control over a group of around 10 men in the 2nd (recruit) company, and I was responsible for their training. There were four groups in every platoon, and four platoons per company. I wasn't particularly happy about this new job because, as a 23-year-old, I now had to give orders to men that were older than me, some of them in their 40s. And since they were also totally hard-nosed about it, I had some difficulties. While around three guys my age – I developed a good camaraderie with one of them named Willi – were almost happy to participate in training, the older guys were rather lazy. It was pretty bad with one of the former prisoners, who probably thought he didn't have to be ordered around by me. When I had the groups line up, he came shuffling along as the last one, and provokingly repeated, "Relax, relax."

When I explained how to shoot a rifle, he would stand around looking bored, as if none of it concerned him. After he then got two other older guys involved, Willi

MEMBERS OF THE SS-SONDERBATAILLON "DIRLEWANGER" IN BELARUS.

MEMBERS OF THE MOTORCYCLE PLATOON FROM THE SS-Sonderbataillon "Dirlewanger."

came to me. He saw that I was overstrained and said, "You have to do something. He's playing games with you." But what was I to do? I went to my platoon leader, who was also a former poacher. He just shrugged his shoulders and had no advice for me. So then I went to the company leader, *Hauptsturmführer* Stöweno. He knew the type I was dealing with, since he had come directly from duty at a concentration camp, and he said to me, "Just punish the guy until he begs for mercy." It didn't take long for the situation to arise. I told him with an almost quivering voice that he should report to me after duty in field dress.

He came along languidly, as usual, but only in his service uniform, and without his steel helmet, combat pack, shovel, etc. I told him "report back to me in 10 minutes in the proper field dress uniform." He mumbled a "kiss my ass" and plodded away. But after 10 minutes he actually returned, and I announced to him that I would carry out a special exercise with him due to his lax approach to duty. He could hardly believe it. My insecurity disappeared relatively quickly, and I began to get louder and louder, "Get down, get up, march, march, get down, get up, march, march, get down! Attention! Forward, march, march. Enemy aircraft on your right. Get up, march, march, enemy aircraft on your left. Attention! Now sing!" Hesitant at first, the man followed my orders. Then he noticed that it would last longer and longer if he didn't do it correctly. Up to now it had worked to some degree, so now I screamed, "Go! Make like a rabbit!" He didn't understand. "Let's go you pussy! Make like a rabbit!" My voice began to crack. I ran up to him and screamed in his face, "Let's go you scoundrel! Rifle in front and hop!" Now I had him where I wanted him. He couldn't take much more. I shouted at him in a stream, "Aw, Mr. Hooligan can't take any more? Maybe Mr. Hooligan would like to go back to the concentration camp? Come on you bastard, now show me you can move!" The longer it went on, the bigger I became. By now, a few curious members of the battalion had stopped in the yard to look on. Since things weren't much different in the other groups: I was setting an example with this.

That evening, Willi came by and said, "Hey, the old man says he's gonna pay you back for that. The first chance he gets, he's gonna shoot you in the back." Oh well. How should I handle it now? I went to *Hauptsturmführer* Stöweno again. He told me he would talk to Dirlewanger about these general problems. And actually, in the next few days, an order followed which pointed out that all newly arrived men had to obey their superiors at all times.

Disobeying this order would mean severe penalties, and even a return to a concentration camp. In August 1943, around 50 men were actually brought back to the concentration camp, including my special friend. Because some of the thugs had already begun to gut civilians and plunder houses, and sending stuff back home right away, they had to start preparing their packages in the office.

It was unbelievable – these guys had only been here for two weeks and they were already stealing things on a daily basis! Since we weren't involved in any front line operations, a large part of the battalion participated in partisan operations starting at the end of July 1943. Those who didn't take part in the operation remained in Lahoysk Palace, or in one of four wooden bunkers in the vicinity to secure the area. The operations were carried out in such a way that we marched into the area in columns and controlled individual villages there. I don't think it made a difference anymore whether the village was a suspected partisan holdout or classified as an enemy of the partisans. We went into a village, which was usually vacated by the residents at the last minute, and secured all of the livestock and food. If villagers were detained, the order came from the company commander whether they were to be sent to a work camp or be liquidated. The villages, almost without exception, were burned to the ground every time. I don't remember how it was decided whether the people were shot or not. I assume that during the debriefing sessions in the run up to the operations it was decided from the commander side which villages should be evacuated or liquidated.

The career criminals behaved like pigs, and went into houses just to see if there was anything to plunder. If any residents got in their way, they were simply mowed down. Only after this would the cattle and crops be collected, loaded up on the *panje* wagons, and brought back with us. These operations were really starting to bother me. In the past I may have still seen the point in it, but these Russians, at least from my perspective, didn't pose any risk to us. A lot of them surely suffered enough under Stalin and the partisans. I told my buddy Willi, who raised his eyebrows and said, "What do you want to do about it then?" I went to Stöweno and explained to him that these operations were killing me. He grimaced, and said "these operations are ordered from the Higher SS and Police Leader, and the orders have to be carried out." To this I replied, "Fighting against the partisans and even partisan sympathizers I can understand, but burning villages and shooting residents without any apparent reason is weighing heavy on me." Stöweno answered that I was not seeing the whole picture, and a command is a command. "You can't decide for yourself what is right and what is wrong." But he also said if a job came up somewhere in Lahoysk and I was replaced, I could go.

I told my buddy Willi this, and he said he would keep an ear to the ground and, of course, come with me. Willi ended up in a concentration camp after repetitive drug use and committing criminal offenses to finance his addiction. But apart from that, he was a good friend that I could depend on. The behavior of the other members of the battalion can be described as follows: everyone did what they wanted. Maybe the same was true of the *landsknechts* during the Middle Ages. The only time there was any order was during the morning and evening roll call, because everyone actually lined up in rank and file. During the day, supervision was rarely possible. Soldiers took every opportunity to organize things that benefited their own personal well being. It went so far that all unpleasant jobs were delegated to Russian civilians, whether it was cleaning rooms, washing clothes or preparing *muckefuck* (a coffee substitute) and food. The troop's food came from Minsk, actually, but it was usually mixed up in the population, except for the coffee substitute.

Fall arrived, and the Red Army became active again – the winters always belonged to them. They were able to break through the German front at Newel, and we engaged in a large partisan combat operation in the hinterlands near the front lines. Due to a lack of German security forces in the area surrounding Rossony, which resembled a primeval forest, a so-called partisan republic formed there. The partisans acted entirely under their own direction and organized a Soviet regime once again – certainly the people there weren't thrilled about it.

Deployment to the Front Lines near Polatsk

We were alerted at the end of October 1943 and placed under command of the combat group "von Gottberg," which consisted mainly of police and had assembled in the Polatsk area. Aside from a work commando in Lahoysk, all units – three German and two Russian companies – were located in the staging area. In winter-like weather conditions, with strong snowfall at times, it was not so pleasant. But in the meantime, we had received winter clothes and now had padded pants and jackets. On November 1, 1943, the order to go into action followed, and we rode on sleighs to the assigned villages and forests. Heavy gun battles with partisans ensued. No comparison to previous operations. The partisans were prepared for our attack and had dug out numerous positions. They also had a great number of artillery cannons and mortars. The weather alone put us at a severe disadvantage here, and the road conditions were a drawback for those who were on the move.

There were some wounded in my group too, and three men were brought to the SS military hospital in Minsk. Our operation against the partisans ended soon because the Red Army was advancing westward from Newel and closing in from the north and south near Dretun. On one hand, I was thinking "Oh crap! Now you're going to die." On the other hand, I thought, "Finally, an operation against regular enemy troops." The entire combat group "von Gottberg" was ordered to go east to take up positions on the front. But some of us had to stay back and do some recon so that we wouldn't be surprised by the partisans, who were everywhere here. Without direct contact with the enemy, we dug our positions. We were supposed to set up a second line, but it wasn't easy in the frozen ground, and we could only dig around one meter deep. We used the excavated dirt to increase our cover. We lay barbed wire in front of us and built wooden bunkers embedded halfway in the ground in exposed positions and behind positions. Equipped with Hindenburg lights and small stoves, they offered shelter from the wind and the weather for up to 20 men, as well as protection from enemy fire. But there were also direct hits, and then the logs went flying around. In a light snowfall, the groups were ordered to take turns in the trenches for 24 hours at a time. You could say that the members of our battalion were very diligent here. It seemed that the criminals could be useful after all, but they always had to be kept busy. Freedom always led to new offenses, which were only punished in exceptional cases.

These guys, who normally acted like ruffians, suddenly showed nerve in this situation. When a group was supposed to carry out a reconnaissance patrol in front of our position, they were shot at. The men ran back immediately and almost caused a panic, because everyone thought that the Red Army was about to attack. But nothing happened. One of Dirlewanger's deputies, *Hauptsturmführer* Weisse, had one of the men court-martialed and shot for it. I have no idea if he was allowed to do that in his position. Weisse had arrived in the *SS-Sonderkommando* in the summer of 1943, after he had beaten a recruit so badly that he died. He came from the Ore Mountains I think, and spoke in a Saxon dialect. Today, you would probably say that he was a complex man because his behavior was absolutely brutal. Weisse had served in a concentration camp before the war, and then went to the SS Totenkopf Division. They must have been happy to get rid of this pig. I don't understand why he wasn't convicted differently for abusing a subordinate. He even kept his rank. He had connections for sure.

I Shoot Down an Airplane

A sewing machine (light Soviet night bomber) approached every evening, stopped its engine before our positions, and sailed over us as a reconnaissance flight. As a farewell greeting from Moscow, the pilot always threw two hand grenades out, but they probably never caused any damage, because they never landed where he was aiming. Behind our positions, he started the engine again and buzzed away. One day I said to Willi, "Someone has to be able to shoot that thing." It always came sailing along from the same direction, and if it was a clear night, you could see it sparkling in the moonlight. Willi shrugged his shoulders and said, "As long as no one minds if you suddenly let loose with the machine gun at night." I went to Stöweno, who granted me permission, and even wanted to be there when it happened. At around 9 p.m. we stood at our post, where Willi and I had improvised a rest for the machine gun. The Rata appeared. It was barely audible. It switched off its engine and came sailing by slowly. I pulled the trigger and fired the first belt at the enemy scout. Since every 10th shell in the belt had a tracer, you could see the flight path of the bullets. After firing, Willi quickly inserted a new belt and I continued. I was hitting the right spot. You could see the bullet holes in the "lame duck." I must have hit the pilot, because he didn't throw any grenades and he didn't restart the engine. The little airplane sailed a bit farther, and then crashed quite harshly in the trees behind our positions. *Hauptsturmführer* Stöweno congratulated me and reported the shooting to Weisse. Probably to show what a battle-worthy bunch he had under him, he reported the success to our authority, the SS Police Regiment 24, who passed on the report to the combat group headquarters. Anyway, Willi and I received a certificate of recognition for it. And shortly after, I was appointed to SS *Rottenführer*. Well, at least it was more money.

We Line Up for a Counterattack

After the skimpy front line that we had set up, our positions had to be improved. Civilians were enlisted to help. They cut down trees and transported them to us. We built wooden bunkers, too – very important, since it was so damned cold. The Russian winter is incomparable to the European winter. After the attacking momentum of the Red Army had subsided, we received the order to counterattack in the middle of November 1943. One evening, our company commander, Stöweno, came to the positions and informed us that we would line up the next morning around 5:30 a.m. in a somewhat distant village. To the left and right of us other companies in our battalion were going, and we were supposed to keep pace by all means. The platoon leader went through at 4:30, woke up the remaining soldiers, and said that we should all be in our positions shortly after 5 am. I went out with Willi a bit earlier and observed the space in front of us. The entire area we had moved into around the forests and lakes was completely foggy. The cold quickly crept into our sleepy limbs and an eerie calm prevailed. I constantly looked at my watch, and then I sent Willi into the bunker to bring the group out. Fortunately, this also went off without a sound. However, I warned everyone again not to light any cigarettes now, to fix their bayonets, and to get their hand grenades ready to throw.

Just before 5:30, Stöweno came and said that we should all proceed in line formation, and as soon as a fixed path in the local area was present, we should then get into an attack formation. It was still so foggy that no one would be able to see us that easily. We cautioned everyone again to keep quiet and then went over the parapet and on our way. Everything remained quiet. We walked through the fog, and many sank into the loose snow. Suddenly, we were standing about 30 meters away from the village. We were speechless. Everything was calm there, and we didn't see a soul. The dug-out positions were unoccupied – Ivan was probably still sleeping in the cottages. We paused for the time being, and Stöweno sent scouts to the left and to the right. They quickly disappeared into the fog. Suddenly, the slow Russian machine guns began to click and the village before us came to life. One company, which had approached to the right of us, was already stepping up to attack this one-horse town. Now we had to go, too. We ran as fast as we could the last few meters and I shouted, "Go! Get in the huts!," and I ran as the first into the nearest cottage. There was a hectic hustle and bustle. Ivan had actually been sleeping. In a mind-boggling stink, there were surely 20-30 Red Army soldiers in the cottage together with their families. I just started shooting around with my sub-machine gun. In the darkness that dominated inside, you couldn't see much anyway. I heard shooting in the other cottages, too. The surprise attack was successful. I shined my flashlight around. Terrified faces and numerous Russians lying around.

I left two men in the cottage and stepped out of the little house with the others to get an overview of the situation. There I could see Red Army soldiers storming out of the other houses which had not been reached by us yet, and they began shooting. We took cover immediately and fired back. There were gun blasts all around us – in the huts near us and behind us, and in the area in front of us. I said to Willi, "Stay here with the others and fire everything you've got. I'll try to quiet things behind us." I went to the next cottage and looked through the window, but I couldn't see anything. I ran to the door and shouted, "Everyone out! I'm throwing a hand grenade!" Two men came running out, and I threw a hand grenade into the house. I shouted, "Go people! Run to the others!," and pointed the way for them. I ran to the next house and repeated the procedure. Then I was on the lookout for the other groups in our company. It was still quite dark outside. I jumped to the next group. "Throw hand grenades into the huts to keep them quiet." Then I saw Stöweno running around with the company troops, and I walked over. He asked me where my group was and I showed him, "There in the front, *Hauptsturmführer.*" "Good," he said, "now let's charge." I nodded, ran back, and when I was with my group I screamed, "Charge! Let's march, march!," and we ran up to the last houses in the village. The other groups charged behind me and next to me, and with a loud "Charge!" shout, we ran up to the shooting Red Army soldiers. They chickened out and fled away from us into the forest. Stöweno came and said that our platoon should get into position immediately and clear out the other houses.

We expected a counterattack by the enemy, so we tried to build defensive positions as quickly as possible. Because the houses would take the hit, we tried to do this on the periphery. But the ground was frozen and it wasn't so easy. We used wood or stone to assist us. Dispatchers ran to each company, and then Stöweno went through our ranks. After this initial success, *SS-Brigadeführer* von Gottberg, who together with three police regiments had command over us, gave the order to push forward. This was a crappy idea actually, because we had to cross through the forest and the marshland to the next village, which could be several kilometers away. I ordered my group to set up a chain of riflemen and to follow me. And so we ran after the fleeing Russians. On the way, we found a few wounded Red Army soldiers who had been abandoned by their comrades. Dispatchers came and encouraged us to hurry, and we kept running. At the same time, the baggage train moved into the just-occupied village and attended to our wounded and brought supplies. The captured Red Army soldiers and civilians were handed over to the SS Police Regiment 24, who had command over us.

We ran and ran through the forest, and didn't see anything but trees and snow. Around noon, a dispatcher appeared and gave us the order to assemble. Apparently, the Russian lines were only thinly occupied here. While the companies gathered, a few reconnaissance patrols were sent out. They were to scout the area and prevent the main group from falling into a trap or an unknown enemy position. Intensified exchange of fire indicated that we could expect new positions. We were dealing with either artillery positions or supply points in the forest. We were brought farther forward, and after a short provisioning, we encountered the targets in the forest. In contrast to the morning, when the element of surprise was on our side, the enemy was now prepared and also had heavy weapons, such as mortars and the rip-boom. We were under heavy fire, and walking almost uncovered through the snow was strenuous. Huge fountains of snow and earth rose among us, and we lost a lot of men. What choice did we have? Wait for spring to come? We couldn't proceed through the forest in tanks either, so the grenadiers were all we had left. Some of our mortars and machine guns reached their positions and shot at the enemy – this boosted morale a bit, at least, but it had little effect. We were nailed to the ground. We tried to crawl forward and throw hand grenades. It was not a good situation. Then the order to charge was given. Again it was, "Charge! March! March! March with a hurrah!" This was probably our only chance to make headway here. Screaming hurrah had a liberating effect. We screamed and ran, shot, and tried not to stumble. They were in a fortified forest camp, similar to what we had seen during the partisan operations. We threw all of the hand grenades we still had, jumped into the trenches, and then over them into the actual camp. During this battle, our weapons were out-matched by the Russians. Almost all of them had automatic weapons, while we charged in with only Karabiners.

In this case, though, the momentum of attack helped us, and after a short dogfight most of the Russians surrendered or sought salvation on the run. Apparently, these guys had little motivation here. Many of them had been forcibly recruited, and were just thrown on the front lines without any special training. We searched the camp, and also found copious food supplies. The *panje* wagons from the baggage train were brought over, and everything was loaded up. It seemed like plundering. The camp consisted of quite a number of ground bunkers, where we also found Red Army soldiers, and even partisans. One of the Red Army soldiers was particularly flustered and kept showing a permit for defectors. Was he really a Stalin objector? In any case he, in particular, was interrogated. What unit did he belong to? Who was in command of the unit? How long had he been here in the area? Where was he drafted? Where was he trained? How strong was the Red Army here? And how was the morale? He chattered on busily and repeatedly rolled cigarettes in newspaper of the *Prawda*. Suddenly, we heard that our company commander, *Hauptsturmführer* Stöweno, had been killed during the battle. Not that it affected us that much, but it was still something unusual when the company commander fell, as compared to any old probation soldier who no one really knew. Stöweno had previously been a commander in a concentration camp, and came to us in the summer of 1943. He hadn't performed any special heroic deeds, but he did lead the company in a relatively respectable manner during operations.

I had also been grazed by a bullet on my upper arm, but it didn't hurt that bad. Luckily the bone wasn't injured, and maybe the cold had a pain-relieving effect. My white padded jacket was covered in blood, so I took up the rear on the way back to the village we had stormed the day before. A battlefield hospital was set up in one of the cottages. All of the dead Russians were collected near the huts – not a pretty site. Our fallen soldiers lay in front of the huts. From the village to our former positions and farther beyond that, there was a bustling horse and cart operation. Little by little the injured and the dead were brought back; weapons, ammunition, and materials were transported forward.

I was told to strip to the waist. I got a shot, and then I was briefly examined. The doctor – he was probably from the SS Police Regiment 24 – said I would be transported to the military hospital. I asked if it was bad, and the doctor answered that it didn't look too bad, but he couldn't do anything else for it here. In the hope that it really wasn't anything bad, I waited for my transport. When someone wanted to put two more corpses on our *panje* wagon – we were around eight men – I told them to forget it and put the dead on the next wagon. The ride back was quite bumpy and slow, and in the meantime, it had become dark again. Eventually we were reloaded onto a truck in a bigger town and brought to a train station. From there we traveled through the night to Minsk, which we reached in the morning. There were trucks waiting to bring us to the SS hospital. In total, there were probably 150 to 200 injured there, but they were from police units, not from our battalion.

Probably around 35 men from our bunch were recovering in hospitals. I stayed in Minsk for close to a week. My wounds were stitched up, and then I was ordered to report in Lahoysk. That was the end of November 1943. A few days after arriving there, Battalion Sergeant Strumpf handed me a certificate and the black Wound Badge. The military hospital had declared me fit for field duty, and I was supposed to do light work for three more weeks. This was certainly more pleasant than being in action. I went to a sauna every day (saunas are found everywhere in Russia). It was operated by three Russians – two of whom were women – and it was a wonderful diversion in this weather.

In Lahoysk, there was only one company from our battalion protecting the town and the palace. The others were in action. The sergeant usually ordered me to the wooden bunkers located around the palace. Since they were well heated with little iron stoves, it was a relatively agreeable job. The purpose of it was to ward off any possible partisan invasions. Luckily, it never came to that.

By mid-December 1943, I was considered fit for military action again, and was ordered to the front near Polatsk, along with other recuperating soldiers. The positions there had been moved farther forward, and the Red Army's incursion area was smaller. Because enemy resistance had stiffened and our own forces had become weaker from the fierce battles, the original position could no longer be established. In fact, winterproof positions were developed and moved into. Neither we nor the enemy carried out further attacks. For two months we sat in our forest positions northeast of Polatsk, and then we were ordered to go back to Lahoysk.

The morale was good. We had fulfilled our mission to stabilize the gaps at the front. The members of the battalion had handled themselves satisfactorily. In all, 50 men had been killed and around 130 injured in the last 14 weeks.

IN PURSUIT OF PARTISANS.

Back in Lahoysk, there were no new operations for the time being. The battalion rested and equipment was repaired; formal training continued and operational capability was reconditioned. The career criminals, who had been with us now for over half a year, had complied quite respectably – at least no one had to worry about being beaten or feared for his life. While plundering had been the primary objective the first time around, now it was comfort and laziness. They passed any job they could on to a Russian. Whether it was cleaning rooms or the police station, washing laundry, heating, or any similar job, it was done by an increasing army of civilians. But now they also received payment for it, in the form of food and cigarettes.

When it became more spring-like, large partisan combat operations between Lepel and Polatsk followed. Here, behind the approaching front lines, there were several bands of partisans who now had to be controlled in order to secure supply lines to the front. In early 1944, this was still possible with strong forces. In this case, numerous troops from the 3rd Panzer Army also participated. In total, there were almost 20,000 men engaged on the German side – roughly the size of two divisions. It was believed that the partisans numbered around 15,000 men, and the populace was mostly partisan friendly.

Most of the transport routes in this area – roads, railways and bridges – were already destroyed or became destroyed on a regular basis. Repair was rarely possible, since the railway engineers or the troops from the OT (Todt Organization) were always attacked by the partisans. And when a road was navigable again, it would be destroyed a few days later. Those posted in their wooden bunkers could be happy when they weren't being blown to smithereens, which happened often enough. The partisans had become incredibly strong. At night, airplanes constantly dropped supplies, as well as heavy weaponry. There were even some field landing strips. Officers of the Red Army were dropped off to train and lead the partisans, and some regular Red Army soldiers were assigned to partisan units.

Before the operation, the ground rules were announced to us by Dirlewanger. In addition to taking out armed partisans, the entire area behind the front lines was to be cleared. All civilians fit for work were to be collected in detention camps. Partisans were to be killed or, in exceptional cases, also collected in detention camps.

In this huge area, only women with small children, the elderly, and invalids in specific villages far away from any transportation infrastructure would remain behind. Anything useful, such as horse carts, food, and livestock, were to be seized. Everything else was destroyed. After knowing how the situation on the front in this area had been since autumn, we were convinced of the importance of this mission. Our mood was good. We had just successfully passed a mission on the front lines, and had rested up for almost two months.

In mid-April 1944, we marched away from Lahoysk. In front was our motorcycle infantry platoon, then a truck with us Germans, and finally the Russians on *panje* wagons. Only a small work commando with around 50 men remained in Lahoysk. Our battalion was under the command of the SS Police Regiment 24, like it was in

"SECURING" CROPS AND LIVESTOCK BECAME AN IMPORTANT PART OF OPERATIONS.

the fall of 1943. As before, all units assembled around the area and then went forward concentrically. The villages were surrounded and searched. There was no action in the first two days. Then, we encountered units in partisan positions, and the first battles ensued. It usually involved embedded wooden bunkers and artillery positions. But we also found real concrete bunkers, where so much sand was used that they didn't harden correctly and offered just as little protection as a wooden bunker against artillery fire.

Because the location was always unfamiliar – the enemy was now able to pull back or line up for a counter attack at any moment – reconnaissance patrols were regularly scheduled. There were mine explosions on several occasions, because the engineers had not yet cleared the forward route. It was always a dull blast. Dirlewanger was pretty hot about it, and called the partisans cowardly pigs. Infuriated, he ordered civilians to march in front of us, as he had done in previous operations. I was once ten meters away when an old Ivan had his leg ripped off by a mine. Glad that it didn't get one of us, I thought. The other locals were paralyzed with terror, and would only continue on after being threatened with a gun. On one trip a woman screamed at us, completely hysterical. "Maltschi (Shut up)" we yelled – to no avail. One soldier was so irritated by it that he aimed his Karabiner at her. She dropped like a tree and began to moan. We said to the others "Fperjott (Forward)," and they trotted along reluctantly.

There were times when we would take fire all of a sudden and would have to take cover and pull back. Now we knew that the enemy was here. By the time the company got close, though, they could already be somewhere else. Trails usually showed us the way to hidden camps. They were set up in the forest with so-called earth bunkers, and were difficult to recognize with the tall undergrowth. There were even saunas there. Hand grenades in and done. The farther we advanced, the more empty villages we found – usually only the elderly and the sick were there, if that. In accordance with our instructions, the villages were burned down. Sometimes, when there was good road access, people were deported back; in rough terrain, liquidation was carried out on the spot, as before. The same with the food – as long as it could be carted off, it was taken care of; otherwise it was burned along with the houses.

Heavy battles broke out several times during the operation, but casualties on our side were kept within limits. I think we had around 20 killed in action and 60 injured. The operation ended in early May 1944, and we went back to Lahoysk for a short time. Here I was appointed to *SS Unterscharführer*.

"Social Misfits" from Concentration Camps as Battalion Reinforcements

In mid-May 1944, we were moved to Uzda, which is about 50 km southwest of Minsk. We stayed in an old military barracks, and in early June 1944, a second battalion was installed to form the *SS-Sonderregiment* "Dirlewanger." Around fifty men, including myself, were assigned to take over training and to lead a platoon of around forty to fifty men. Major Steinhauer of the police force, who had beforehand led an artillery battery with Russian volunteers, became battalion commander. They had already been with us for a long time. He stayed with us until the war's end, and I later heard that he had been missing since the last days of the war. Maybe he went into hiding, like many others. My company commander was now *Obersturmführer* (Senior Assault Leader) Gast, an administrative officer who could enter invoices, but possessed zero qualities as a tactical leader.

Then, two transports arrived in Uzda by rail, with a total of about 500 new probation troops (already in uniform) from the concentration camp. We received them at the train station and marched with them to Sabolotje, situated to the southwest. There the men were divided up, and we were now inserted as group and platoon leaders. We already had plenty of experience with the career criminals who had come to us a year ago and knew how to handle the new arrivals. As *Unterscharführer* with a few decorations, my authority was to be respected. Dirlewanger, who was often in Berlin to sort out organizational issues about increasing his unit, returned by plane a few days later and addressed the new arrivals. While doing so, he pointed his finger at us and said that we were also once probation troops who had already been rehabilitated and distinguished ourselves on the battle field. He told them to seize this opportunity to make up for their past mistakes and become respectable soldiers. Those who didn't comply, though, would return from where they came.

I had been overwhelmed by the situation a year ago, so this time I showed the new guys how the rabbit runs straight away. I conferred with the group leaders of my platoon and told them that they should clamp down immediately if someone didn't toe the line. Because they had already been *kapos* in a concentration camp, they knew how to get by such guys. The new probation troops were almost all social misfits. These were people who were unemployed in Germany and wouldn't take work that the employment office assigned to them three times. Thus, they were considered indolent and committed to forced labor in a concentration camp. A former *kapo*, who had been with us since July 1943 and now served as squad leader with one stripe (platoon leaders had two stripes and company commanders three) on the forearm of his field blouse, said to me, "These guys are all dirt bags and they'll shirk responsibility wherever they can." And this is actually the impression that we got, too.

To counter this, we led a strict regiment. If I didn't get an immediate response when I made an appearance somewhere, for example, I made one or all of them do drills until he or they could no longer stand up. Before that they were yellow, and now it was much better.

Like we did a year before, we had to teach the new recruits everything: basic training with lining up in a row and march formation, marching in step and about face, exercises with the rifle, saluting, orientation in terrain, setting up field posts and stations, attacking enemy positions, defending positions, shooting theory, etc.

Retreat from Belarus

On June 22, 1944, the Red Army's offensive began. We were all immediately put on high alert. Extensive partisan action was to be expected. Days before the offensive, the partisans had already been quite active. Roads and bridges being blown up in the hinterlands and attacks on smaller supply points were reported several times a day. While the 1st Battalion was commanded by the higher SS and police leaders for the operation, our 2nd Battalion was moved from the approaching front lines to the west. In July 1944, the Red Army was closing in on Minsk, and company-by-company we marched away on foot.

We needed over ten exhausting days for the roughly 250 km march. We were directed to the existing roads through forests, marshes, and rivers. At the company level, we didn't hold enough cards to be able to walk along specific alternatives here. Columns were backed up several kilometers at rivers, like the Nemen.

We stood around and nothing moved, and enemy strafers came again and again and shot at the columns. But if a 2 cm anti-aircraft gun was available, they turned away quickly. Then they had respect. Along the access roads to the bridges there were several anti-tank guns to protect us from surprise attacks. Everyone's nerves were on edge here. We wanted to get away from here at all costs, but we couldn't, because the columns weren't moving. I said to my company commander, "*Obersturmführer*, should I go ahead and see how long the traffic jam is and possibly look for an alternative?" Gast took his cap off, scratched his head, and said, "Ok, go ahead. But be back in one hour at the latest."

In front of us, every unit was represented: medical units, farming leaders, *Landesschützen* battalions (land troop battalions), rear field units, and OT units. I couldn't get forward up to the bridge, which was in the city Nowy Swierzen. I could tell already that it would take hours, because at the moment it was at a standstill. I went back to Gast and said, "We won't make it over the bridge anytime soon. There might be another chance with our vehicles near Stolpce, but it's probably the same there." The only possibility would have been to leave the vehicles here and try to swim over the river, which was about 120 meters wide here. Of course, Gast rejected that idea. He wanted to wait until things got moving again. Afternoon came, then evening, and night. And we were still standing.

After a few men had wandered off, Gast was very agitated and threatened us platoon leaders with court martial if we didn't prevent it. But I couldn't possibly run after every guy when he slipped away during the day or at night.

At night, things started to move all of a sudden – the *panje* horses pulled forward, but after half an hour we were standing still again. There was no command available, and the men split up to protect the columns from partisans. I didn't want to do that with our nitwits. We were the last company to march out of Uzda, and were also at the end of the line here. Units merged in front of the bridge from both sides, and as a result we lost the direct connection to the other companies. Finally, we stood just before the bridge and had to stop again. The other units were already over. Gast went to the field gendarmerie, who was supposed to control everything in front of the bridge, and wanted to send a man over to at least inform the battalion that we weren't over yet. "They notice," was the answer – no one was allowed over.

Knowing that the Russians were at our backs was not a good feeling. When we marched over the bridge the next day, there was no sign of our battalion anywhere. No scouts and no information board, nor any other kind of notification. Gast came to me and said, "Look for the battalion. Organize some sort of transportation and go." Behind the bridge, the whole column fanned out in four or five or more directions in order to advance more quickly. Everyone wanted to get away as fast as possible, and we anticipated encountering more bottlenecks through bridges or even marshes. When a motorcyclist came by, I waved him down to stop. I told him to take me with him because I was looking for the battalion for our company. He motioned for me to get on, and we roared along the columns to the city Mir. At first I didn't recognize anything among the many columns. Because it backed up again, I had him stop. I got out and thought "there is no way the battalion made it this far, and if I just walk around the entire space, I will find the other companies."

Then, I actually saw our bucket car in the middle of the columns with the battalion commander, as well as adjutants and squad leaders, already standing again and waiting to pass through to the city. Behind them, around 500 meters apart, the individual companies, with each group trudging along behind one or two *panje* wagons carrying baggage and some footsore soldiers. I wriggled my way through the columns, announced my presence, and said that the Gast Company was about 20 km behind the battalion. Steinhauer said he couldn't step out of line here and wait for the company. On the contrary, Gast should try to join up somehow. He gave me one of his three dispatch riders, who brought me back.

We drove along the dusty columns and looked for the company intensely. Actually, we had to drive for about 25 minutes on the motorcycle to find them. It probably would have taken four hours on foot. I told the driver "wait a minute," on the edge of the road, and went to the company commander. After my report, he wanted to be driven to Steinhauer himself to discuss the company joining up, and he handed responsibility of the men over to me as platoon leader. Well, I didn't have to do much. Everyone just trudged westward. After around an hour, Gast was brought back by the motorcyclist. He had received a map from Steinhauer and now wanted to try to find an alternative route to meet up with the battalion again.

Because the Red Army was advancing rapidly, this idea certainly wasn't a bad one. We didn't want to be bombarded. While the masses were jammed up in front of Mir, Gast decided to pull the company out to the right and march to the north over smaller trails, then turn to the west and advance behind Mir to the battalion. This probably lasted over five hours, but we were able to keep moving while the rest stood still. When we saw Mir off to our left, we went over the Miranka River near a small village, and Gast sent me ahead with two men to find the battalion. We walked at a fast pace to the southwest, and from a distance we could already see the columns piled up again – the Nemen had to be crossed here again. Because we had sidestepped on smaller paths, we arrived so quickly that we were even ahead of our battalion. The three of us went southeast along the columns and found our guys, who had just come through Mir. Steinhauer was surprised to see us coming from the front and asked where our company was. I told him, and after briefly mulling it over he said he would send the three dispatch riders with me. The Gast Company was to wait for the battalion, but we were to find alternative routes toward Navahrudak with the dispatch riders. Soon we would all be together again.

We drove along the columns and met up with our company again. I reported to Gast, who spread out the map and lost his cool. "Dammit!" he screamed agitatedly. "To the west there is only marshland. We'll lose even more time!" A branch of the Nemen, in particular, still had to be crossed there – impossible in the marshes without a solid bridge. But according to the map, there weren't even any small villages. In order to carry out the command, he gave me the order to try to go along the road and over the tributary with the three dispatch riders and two company members, and then, as soon as the marsh ended, to find a side route ahead of Navahrudak that the battalion could march ahead on. If necessary, I should set up posts or send a dispatch rider back.

He had the Sergeant issue marching orders so we wouldn't be detained at checkpoints, and he gave me the map. Then we were off. Because we rode along on the edge of the columns with solo motorcycles, we advanced quickly and pushed southeast of Karelichy, to the bridge access road. (I can reproduce these place names because I received the map back then, and I left it at the farm during my home leave in October 1944. I still have it today.) The atmosphere was shattering. There was no more "From Finland to the Black Sea, forward, forward, forward, forward to the East we march..." Here, old Landesschützen, women auxiliaries, staff, and other support units moved westward in single file. Sometimes you would see a motor vehicle in between, but most traveled by foot or *panje* wagon. Proper Wehrmacht carts were also a rarity.

We pushed our way through, and someone screamed at the top of his voice, "You'll come back quick enough, you pigs!" It didn't bother us at the time. After the bridge, we drove about 15 km to the next village and confirmed the entries in the map – there were several ways away from the road. Because everything before it was marshland, the battalion first had to meander their way here. It could take six to eight hours, depending on how long the battalion had to wait at the bridge. The clock was ticking. Although we didn't notice it directly and no messages had come through yet, we could feel that the Red Army was advancing quickly. I sent a dispatch rider back to Gast and the battalion, and had the remaining two dispatch riders start the next route. We also met a few units here who were either stationary or were moving toward the road or away from it. I stopped and asked where the unit came from and where they wanted to go. But the small man had no idea, and I didn't need to speak to an officer. We continued in a northwesterly direction.

We could hear the thundering artillery. Planes roared swiftly away above us – they weren't German any more. The driver thumped against the tank. There was still gas in it, but at some point we would have to either refuel somewhere, or at least turn back to the road. The farther we drove the fewer troops we saw. After half an hour through the hilly and increasingly forested landscape, we began to pass company-sized formations, which, like us, probably planned to scrape along to the west on back roads. Eventually, my dispatch rider stopped to take a look at the gas and thought we would only be able to continue for another 10 minutes if we were to make the trip back. I told him to drive the ten minutes. In the meantime, the road veered off in a westerly direction, just like on the map, and it looked as if it were possible to continue west on this side road without slowing. The battalion could manage at least 40 km a day. We left the second motorcycle there and drove farther – this way we at least saved the gas in the other motorcycle. When we passed a small village, I asked an old man if this was the way to Navahrudak. He didn't understand me, and just looked at me with no expression at all – a peculiarity that I had seen so many times with the Russians. I pointed to the west and screamed, "Navahrudak?" He didn't say anything.

We drove on into a forested area, and saw a smaller column with horses and carts ahead of us. Suddenly shots were fired. The column froze. Partisans! My dispatch rider stopped immediately. Spellbound, we stared ahead at the drama that was unfolding there. Three of four men ran to the left, away from the column, in order to reach the forest, but they all dropped after a few meters. We could see partisans coming out of the woods on the right, searching for the column. More single shots were fired. Then my driver turned around, and we drove back at full speed. We could definitely expect partisan attacks here.

We drove back, met the other dispatch rider with the second soldier attached, and drove back to the company. I reported the situation, and Gast said we would now have to wait for the battalion. Luckily, they came marching up shortly after. I passed my report on to Steinhauer, who then had a conversation with Gast. Eventually, Steinhauer decided that we should try to march on the side roads – Ivan was closing in behind us here on the main road. It was a dangerous undertaking due to the partisans, not to mention with men who were only trained fourteen days ago and displayed no particular motivation.

According to the map, it was still around 30 km to Navahrudak. Marching there would take almost 10 hours! The men had to take a break once in a while. It wasn't so bad with the shaggy *panje* horses. The creatures were unbelievably tame, but they needed to take breaks, too. After having had to sleep where they stood during the

THE IMPROVISED RETREAT TO LYCK/EAST PRUSSIA.

long-lasting traffic jam at the bridge, the men were fit enough for these marching demands. Since the entire battalion was supposed to march in a column, the danger of a partisan attack was also lower. Our company took the point; the battalion members and the three other companies followed. We marched on the same road that we had driven by motorcycle, and eventually found the ambushed column. We saw around 35 killed in action here; among them there were also some women who had probably been working with the support crew. The column had been looted. Weapons were gone, shoes were gone, and trunks and laundry bags were all emptied out. Some had shots to the head. Steinhauer had the dog tags and pay books removed from the dead, and the bodies were buried on the side of the road.

Early the next morning, we were north of Navahrudak. Steinhauer sent *Obersturmführer* Gast to the city with the three motorcycles. The field gendarmerie said Grondo was the new target, and mentioned that Ivan had already taken Mir – that was 50 km from us. Around 30 km ahead of us was the Nemen again, which meandered all around in this area. It was still 140 km to Grodno. That meant we still had a day's walk to the Nemen, and the Red Army could get here quickly with tanks. We had to hurry. Luckily, we could then cross the Nemen a few kilometers north of the road. The chaos here was beyond belief. There was a rail line and two roads: one to Lida, like the railway, and one to Grodno. Since so many people wanted to get away as quickly as possible, they tried to get to Lida by train, and from there to Grodno by train. Our 1st Battalion would be engaged in battle in the following days, but we didn't know that at this point.

Anyway, the steady traffic dissipated and we were able to continue marching on the road directly to Grodno without any major roadblocks. Defensive positions were being worked on heavily there. We saw a lot of civilians digging anti-tank ditches. After a short break, and food for the men and the animals, we moved on again toward East Prussia. We marched through Augustow to Treuburg, and stayed in the barracks of an RAD camp there. Little by little, stragglers from our 2nd and 1st Battalions were arriving. Our battalion had arrived from Belarus with almost no losses. We finally had the opportunity to wash ourselves again and shake the dust off our clothes. We could rest up a bit here and get regular meals to eat. After two days, normal operations began again with the training of the men. At the end of July 1944, I received the silver Anti-Partisan Badge. It was probably a prize for my two years of service in Belarus. I wasn't the only one. Practically everyone who had been there since the beginning, and was still living, got one.

Operation during the Warsaw Uprising.

In early August, we were put on high alert. The 1ˢᵗ Battalion, which had been decimated by battles in retreat, was brought to Warsaw by truck the next day. We were all caught off guard and wondered what was happening there, so suddenly. A day later, our 2ⁿᵈ Battalion also received the order to relocate to Warsaw, via Johannisburg and Ostrolenka. We then assumed it was a limited operation against the Polish national resistance army (Home Army), which was holding up well in the forests surrounding Warsaw. More couldn't be expected from our foot soldiers, though.

But then we found out that a rebellion had broken out in Warsaw itself. We were commanded to force our way into the city center to the Wehrmacht headquarters and to quell any resistance. Since we didn't have any training in urban warfare, we just went for it. Coming in from the west, we were to proceed eastward over Litzmannstädter Street to Brühl Palace. After some time, we took infantry fire from houses and barricades. We suffered our first hold-up, as well as our first wounded. Advance, stop, shoot, and take cover. Into homes and breaking resistance, and then just continuing forward! Our probation troops, who had been sitting in a concentration camp eight weeks ago, took heavy losses. One of them was standing right next to me when he took a shot through his steel helmet. I heard "pang," and then he was lying there beside me. I quickly ran to a house entrance. The bullets were flying all around me. The door was locked, but at least the doorway arch gave me a bit of protection. I took a look around me. The other men had also retreated to doorways. Some were already lying in the street. There was no way to advance. We had to get into the houses and eliminate the shooters. Most doors were sealed, so they were broken open with rifle butts or blown up with hand grenades. Once we were in the houses, everything happened rather quickly. We couldn't give the insurgents any time to react. Anyone who was in the house and could have shot at us was taken care of. Other civilians were led away from the city on Litzmannstädter Street and gathered in a detention center.

Little by little, the street was cleared. Our men entered houses in groups, and fifteen or more houses were searched at the same time. It was out of one house and into the next. Then, suddenly, the shooting from the Polish side subsided. Apparently they thought the uprising would be easier.

By midday, though, we had already lost a lot of men. The battles eventually leveled off and the street combat became a little more like routine. At night, we hunkered

THE BATTLE FOR WARSAW BEGINS.

down and were all on high alert. The next day, we walked through market halls to get to Brühl Palace, where the German command and the rest of the 1st Battalion were located. There were still around 50 men! From here, we launched daily attacks in the surrounding streets. Warsaw was burning everywhere. Heavy artillery and aircraft bombarded entire streets and quarters. Bazookas were handed out and fired off into houses and basements without any training.

In mid-August, the next order to attack followed: overpowering Warsaw's Old Town. The old houses, with their thick walls and heavy doors, were all fortresses. There were explosions everywhere. Locating where shots were coming from and who was targeted was impossible. It was pure chance whether you were wounded or not. Gun battles from floor to floor inside a house were not uncommon. Some of the rebels would hole up in cellar rooms and then disappear through underground connections and/or sewers.

Wehrmacht Felons, Turkmen, and SS and Police Convicts

To balance out the high losses, and to be able to continue the assault, we constantly received replacement troops. In addition to more concentration camp prisoners, almost 1,000 Wehrmacht felons came in August. They re-formed the 1st Battalion and also bolstered our 2nd Battalion. Because they arrived in their Navy, Air Force, and Army uniforms, the companies now looked quite colorful. Motivation was non-existent across the board. Apparently, it was not very nice in the Wehrmacht prisons, and now here they were, nothing more than cannon fodder (like us too, I suppose). The commanders didn't care at all how many fell. Maybe they even thought the more, the better – as long as the uprising was being fought. Contingent upon location, the otherwise typical bureaucracy was relinquished and we platoon leaders didn't report at all anymore who was wounded or killed. Instead, we only reported the numbers (how many had been killed or wounded), provided that we could even survey it. Often we only reported troop levels. Who had been killed or was hiding or had defected, was not noted for the time being.

The Turkmen also fought alongside us during the operation, and they were absolutely worthless to us. Even the social misfits from the concentration camp or the Wehrmacht felons were preferred over them. By the end of August, everything was more coordinated. We went district by district, and even the replacements were now properly included. In September, another 1,500 men from the penal system of the SS and Police in Danzig-Matzkau arrived. They filled up the files that had become heavily thinned out again. The majority of the Wehrmacht felons had already been killed, wounded, or had defected somehow. Up to now, I had been lucky. Among the men from Danzig-Matzkau was the demoted Storm Trooper who wrote a book after the war about *SS-Sturmbataillon 500*, under the pseudonym Ingo Petersen. He was already a story teller back then. Counter to his protestations after the war, he was never a Junior Assault Leader or a company commander, and he was never awarded the Knight's Cross or the Iron Cross. I have no idea if he was awarded the EK II before his court martial. In any case, he didn't get it with us. Basically, the guys from Danzig-Matzkau were good. There they had been occupied with breaking in shoes or working for arms manufacturers, among other things. One of them also told me that they had to clean up the rubble after bombing

Operation in a sea of ruins in the Polish capital.

attacks in Danzig. Everything was always double time. They were grateful to get away from there.

When the uprising had almost been defeated, Dirlewanger had a birthday. Gast took me with him to the party. The squad leader Reinefarth, who became mayor of Sylt or Amrum after the war, was also present. Dirlewanger was a man of many faces and was kind of moody. He only had contempt left for entire groups of people; like when the social misfits and the Wehrmacht felons came in, for example. His orders against the partisans, Jews, and other enemies had been pragmatic. His philosophy was that they were enemies, and the fewer there were, the better. But he would also go to bat for those who proved themselves worthy, whether it be with promotions (even an old poacher from Salzburg or Vienna could become *Untersturmführer*), or with rehabilitation requests. He was also generous to us with decorations. As I already mentioned, everyone who had been there since the beginning was awarded the Anti-Partisan Badge. He simply had the Sergeant put all of our names on the award lists. At the birthday party, which began in the early evening and went on into the morning, things got a little out of hand in this regard. Dirlewanger handed Reinefarth lists with names of those who were to be awarded with the EK II or, like me, with the EK I. Reinefarth looked at the lists and said it wouldn't be possible, he only had a limited allotment available. Dirlewanger, who was drunk, as he normally was at these kinds of festivities, got loud and screamed that those who put their necks on the line for others and had answered for the misery would get the recognition they deserved. That was, of course, an affront beyond compare. Reinefarth, who had a totally different demeanor than Dirlewanger, almost aristocratic, left the party with his companions immediately after.

Despite that, Dirlewanger was awarded the Knight's Cross at the end of operations in Warsaw. And apparently it went through, because the award request – from Reinefarth too – was put in before this incident. I actually think that the Knight's Cross award represented a rather general appreciation of Dirlewanger. After all, he managed to integrate all of the probation troops, and then achieved a big success for the German side with them (even though there were heavy losses) by defeating the Warsaw Uprising. Dirlewanger received the Knight's Cross, I got the EK I and leave. When I picked up my leave pass, our Sergeant told me that Gast had also submitted a request for me to become *Oberscharführer* (Senior Squad Leader).

I was full of pride on the trip home. Here I had been labeled a criminal after a silly mistake, and now I was coming back a highly-decorated *Unterscharführer*. I went to the farm on foot from the train station and touched base with the farmer. He still couldn't contain his astonishment. "Well, you have really made something of yourself," he said. "I'll go call your mother." Then he went to the cupboard and took out a bottle of schnapps and two glasses. I was glad, too. "Hey," he said, "let's forget what happened in the past, ok? When the war is over, come back, alright?" The days I spent there were great. My mother came and hugged me straight away.

BAZOOKAS WERE USED FOR CLOSE COMBAT AGAINST ENTRENCHED
REBELS IN WARSAW'S STREETS.

In the demolished city of Warsaw.

She was overjoyed to see me healthy and cheerful, and she was also proud of my new Iron Cross. "So, you can have the day off today," the farmer said, and to me, "Come again tomorrow and tell me about the front, ok?" The fourteen days were wonderful. October revealed its magnificent colors and many sunny days. I even had a little sweetheart. Everything was beautiful. Just before the end of my leave, a telegram came. I was to report again at the concentration camp in Sachsenhausen. This time I wasn't worried about it. I just assumed that I would accompany some prisoners again.

Political Prisoners

Again, I went by train to Berlin, and from there I took the city train to Oranienburg. Nothing had changed, except that there was bomb damage everywhere. I took the foot path from the train station to the concentration camp again. I showed my marching orders and pay book at the gate, and in I went to the office. The Sergeant told me which block I was to report to. There I met some fellow soldiers who had also been sent on leave after the Warsaw operation. We were actually supposed to take prisoners with us again, and then bring them to the replacement company in Krakow. This time they were mainly political prisoners, but judging by their badges, there were also career criminals (green triangle) and social misfits (black triangle). They wore their blue and white striped prison uniforms; or, if they had been *kapos*, civilian clothing. They were able to line up and march – some of them had had to do it for years now – so we started with field training. "Get down! Up and march," etc. Interesting for me was how well fed most of them looked. There were no Muslims among them.

Like the work-shy prisoners we had received the last time, these prisoners were not particularly motivated. But they seemed to be more open than the social misfits. Little by little, the equipment arrived. This mainly included worn-out uniforms and used boots. The guys received an SS pay book, and were also photographed for it. Most still had shaved heads in the pictures. We stayed at the concentration camp in Sachsenhausen for around four weeks. It was a little strange eating in the officer's canteen – we were once prisoners here ourselves, if only for a short time. Since then, we had climbed in rank to become officers, some of us highly-decorated, and now we ate in the canteen with officers of the military command and guard battalion. It wasn't just our collar patches that were different, but most of them also wore the ribbon of the War Merit Cross.

We didn't have much contact, though, because we ate at different times. But we saw them more frequently, and in addition to the many crooked characters from Southeastern and Eastern Europe, numerous war invalids stood out. The Sachsenhausen concentration camp itself reduced its guard by about 50 men. They were mostly ethnic Germans who were no longer wanted. They didn't speak pure German and, to me, they were not that bright. After about a week I was ordered to the office, where I received the promotion to *Oberscharführer*. I had to acknowledge, and the Sergeant told me that I should go to the storeroom and pick up a couple of stars and new shoulder straps.

The security guards of the concentration camp were used as squad leaders, and they were visibly peeved about it. They came together as much as they could and left the prisoners alone. Even though it was understandable, it wasn't allowed. We troop commanders had to remind them repeatedly. In early November, we were then transported to Krakow by train. Our replacement company was housed in part of a convent. Contact with the nuns was forbidden. We were afraid that one of these guys would try to get into their panties. We saw them occasionally rushing around in their black frocks, but apart from those who shared use of the convent's kitchen, contact was limited. We realized, however, that a few of the nuns spoke some German. During the two weeks in Krakow, the men were trained further and the training was reduced to the essentials. First, they were trained to use weapons, which included mainly Italian rifles. Interestingly, the political prisoners presented us the fewest difficulties. We had a bad feeling about the professional criminals; with the "social misfits" and the Wehrmacht felons it was more just mutual contempt. We really had to push this lazy bunch.

In mid-November, it was back to the train station again and off to Diviaky, in Slovakia. Headquarters were in a small palace here, and the companies stayed in barns and stables. Bit by bit, several hundred concentration camp prisoners arrived, as did court martialed officers who were inserted as company commanders. I was made platoon leader of the 5th *SS-Sturmregiment 2*. My new company commander was Momm, who had been demoted from colonel to cavalry captain, and had won a medal in the 1936 Olympics as a show jumper. Harry Momm was a small, wiry, and snappy person. He was said to have been an acquaintance of Stauffenberg, and opened a bottle of champagne when the attempted assassination of Hitler was announced. Whether that is true or not, I don't know, because we saw Momm a short time later in the uniform of a *Hauptsturmführer*. He must have changed from the Army to the Waffen-SS. Everyone else tried to prevent it. *Hauptsturmführer* Ehlers became the battalion commander. I think he was removed due to cowardice in the face of the enemy and incompetence in a SS-Division. He had been a commander in the Sachsenhausen concentration camp until the beginning of the war. When our regiment commander, Buchmann, was also removed due to incompetence, *Hauptsturmführer* Momm took over the battalion at the end of 1944 and Ehlers the regiment. Ehlers was supposedly strung in the forest in April 1945 by former concentration camp prisoners in his regiment, probably because he had been so brutal back then. Ehlers came from near Hanover and was only awarded the War Merit Cross 2nd Class. This demonstrated his lack of military skill. He was really slow to take action and was not very well liked. Since we all considered him a weenie, we made a lot of jokes at his expense. It doesn't surprise me that three or four former prisoners hung him up in the last chaotic days of the war.

Establishing the SS-Sturmbrigade "Dirlewanger"

In Diviaky, we now began to set up a brigade. The companies and battalions were brought together, but it was an absolute catastrophe, because it was made up of criminals, social misfits, and other not-particularly-trustworthy contemporaries. Maybe we could have established a reasonably tight unit in three months, on a military training ground shielded from locals of the surrounding area. The really difficult cases would be sent back to concentration camps, like in 1942 and 1943, and those remaining would get used to the new routine.

There were some among the political prisoners who really thought that they were something better. They had their positions in whatever secret, usually communist committees, and still felt that they were qualified for something higher. There were still communist agitators among the prisoners who were punished severely by Dirlewanger and Weisse. Extremely difficult cases were liquidated. So we tried to bring calm to the place. Of course, this was hardly feasible with almost 2,000 new prisoners, and by November the companies were already deployed to the various villages around Diviaky. The area was supposed to be secured, but now the guys were out there with no supervision and of course immediately began to loot the surrounding homes and farms. It wasn't so much the political prisoners, who considered the Slovaks to be friends, but rather the criminals, the social misfits, and the Wehrmacht felons.

As a result, Dirlewanger decided to implement concentration camp style punishments. This mainly included beatings on the backside or on the kidneys. In the concentration camp, it was known as being taken to the whipping post. Here, it was carried out on a table. The rule was 25 blows to the buttocks – sometimes it was only 10. Then they were locked up in the standing bunker, which was made of wood. They weren't able to sit, and had to stand the entire time. After a few hours, the box was opened and the men collapsed limply.

Basically, it can be said that the entire brigade was pretty much useless. At the end of November, we were relocated to the south by train and were supposed to chase down partisans in the mountains. But I think someone just wanted us out of the villages.

The Prisoners Defect

Momm was always asking us platoon leaders how the morale of the company was. He knew what kind of men they were. Even though most of the political prisoners were inconspicuous, there were some among them who were capable of anything. Most of the prisoners only had scorn left for us platoon leaders. We had also been in prison, and had chummed up to the SS and received uniforms and medals in return. The mood was always very tense, and since we were outnumbered we tried not to let things escalate. The ethnic German squad leader from the concentration camp guard detail told us now and then that they suspected so-and-so to be a communist functionary who was inciting the others. But some of the prisoners also tried to get the squad leaders, and even us, on their side. It was always those who displayed a bit more vision. "Man, everything is falling apart here, think about how this is all going to end. In half a year the war is over, and what will you do then? The Russians will bump you off immediately. Maybe you should start to think about alternatives." I always answered that every man has gone his own way, whether he wanted to or not; I wasn't making any accusations, but I also didn't want to go their way.

In early December, we were suddenly moved to the front lines near Ipolysag. Momm thought it would be a fiasco with the men, and we should try to prevent the worst. We were brought to the front by truck and took over a Wehrmacht battalion's positions. It was mainly trenches here, and in the rear were the artillery positions. Relief took place in the evenings and worked out quite well. At night, heavy artillery fire rained down on the positions and we suffered losses. The guys were really freezing outside. It was below zero and the men hadn't received any winter clothing, except for their jackets. They stood in the trenches or warmed up in the wooden bunkers. The Italian carbine was on the breast – there was practically no shooting. We didn't see any Russians. Around dawn, our 3rd Battalion moved into positions near us. Not only had the men all been political prisoners, but the fact that they had only been soldiers for eight weeks raised a lot of doubts for me. Even if they tried, they were no match for the Russians!

Soon afterward, the Russian artillery fire increased, then it stopped, and suddenly we heard tanks starting up. The mood became uneasy. I didn't know how we were supposed to hold back the tanks, if it came to that. We didn't even have any bazookas. The men became more and more unsettled, and I had no idea what I should do, other than urge calm. I walked around between the groups and observed the approach, which didn't lead directly to us, but to the neighboring 3rd Battalion. Since blood is thicker than water, I thought: "Thank God they're not coming to us!" Suddenly, there was shooting in our area. I tried to make out what was happening there, because there were no Russians in sight yet. Then I saw it. A few men, and then more and more of them, climbing out of the trenches and running forward through the shot-up barbed wire barriers. What was happening here? Again, there were shots and a few of the running men fell over.

When I turned back around I had a gun in my chest and one of my men asked me, "Are you coming or staying? We're going over to the Russians!" I said, "Hey, don't pull this crap! What are you doing?" He took my gun from me and said, "Give thanks to your God and piss off." Then the men from my platoon also climbed over the edge of the trench, threw their weapons and gear away after a few meters, and ran up to the Russian lines. I stared at the scene in stunned disbelief. I looked around. The positions were practically empty. Two squad leaders looked just as dumbfounded as I did. One was missing. Did he defect too? A few men who didn't want to go over to the Russians were still there, too, and looked at us quizzically. "Go look for weapons together," I ordered, and I tried to sort out the situation. Then I went over to Momm. He still didn't quite realize what had just happened. "Cavalry Captain," I said, "the company has defected and not just ours, possibly the entire battalion!" "What did you say?" he screamed, and ran out of the command post. Just then, the enemy tanks had made it to the positions of our 3rd battalion, to our left. We saw the men walking away from behind. "Oh God," Momm said, and ordered me to sort out how many had deserted from our company. We had about 35 to 40 men left from over 150. To our left, we heard repeated shooting from the tanks. There was no resistance. Then came the order, "Move out!" We took all of the weapons we could find and carry, and pulled back. I was happy to finally get away from the line of fire. I had actually been completely irresponsible to bring a battalion with former prisoners into the HKL (*Hauptkampflinie*, main front). It was pretty close to sabotage! We gathered in a small village behind the front and watched as the armored infantry of the Army rolled by in trucks and infantry fighting vehicles in order to recapture the positions.

Dirlewanger came with Weisse in the bucket car and asked what had happened. He didn't blame those of us in charge, but he did rail against the Army generals who, in his opinion, had intentionally precipitated the situation. He had the company commander give him a report on the troop levels and said, after he had calmed down a bit, "At least the pigs are gone!" With that he expressed his dislike for the KPD members and Social Democrats.

He ordered us to gather the rest and to march to the area near Banska Stiavnica – Krupina. Then he drove on again with Weisse. In total, our 2nd Battalion still had the strength of a company. The 3rd Battalion was said to have about the same. Around 600 former prisoners had deserted to the Red Army. They massacred some of the squad leaders and platoon leaders. In the following days – it was Christmas time – we were interrogated by the SD, and Dirlewanger even came to us again. Accompanying him was a *Hauptsturmführer*, who had been assigned judge for the *Sturmbrigade*, and evidently was also supposed to lead the investigation. Dirlewanger didn't respect him at all. There had previously been a lot of tension between the two, because the *Hauptsturmführer* wanted to adjust the jurisdiction within the brigade according to the military penal code, which Dirlewanger flat out rejected. Actually, this wasn't even possible with our unit. The military penal code had been written to uphold discipline and order in a normal unit. We had only criminals and social misfits, and they were always capable of anything. Forty percent of the men probably would have been sitting in a penitentiary at any given time. It was more pragmatic to implement concentration camp punishments. The guys had respect for beatings.

Christmas, 1944, was the saddest I've ever had. Even in prison we had a big Christmas tree and the prison authorities organized something resembling a party. The rest of our company celebrated Christmas sitting in a Slovakian house in a gloomy mood. Unlike previous years, there were no little presents, no cake, and no nice roast. A few pine branches lay on the table, a few Hindenburg lights burned, and each of us rummaged what we had out of our haversacks. We didn't feel like singing. I shouted, "But we're still alive, guys." Later I visited my pal Willi, who was serving in the 7th Company. He saw me and said, "Everything's gone to hell. Those damned Communist pigs. If I ever see one of them again, I'll shoot him dead!" Willi had a room with another fellow soldier in the home of a Slovakian family, and the three of us sat in the darkness with a tallow candle. The father of the family knocked on the door and brought us something to eat and drink. He spoke passable German and said, "Next Christmas peace!" and we answered, "Yeah, hopefully!"

In the next few days, I was repeatedly questioned. I was supposed to give the names of those I noticed and answer why I didn't report anything, etc. "Now they want to come after me," I thought – they were probably looking for a culprit. But luckily there was no action. I was even threatened with a gun. Maybe they hoped they could capture the deserters again somehow. Maybe if they were to be used against us on the front.

I Become Company Commander

While part of the SS Sturm Regiment 1 was still in action, SS Sturm Regiment 2 assembled in the hinterlands. In total, our regiment had over 1,000 men. Among them, though, there were still about 400 former political prisoners from the 1st Battalion and then a mix of Wehrmacht felons, social misfits, and professional criminals from the concentration camps, as well as previously convicted SS members. The regiment was restructured and our regiment commander was removed for the failure at Ipolysag. I became company commander, Momm was battalion commander, and our previous battalion commander, Ehlers, became regiment commander. A lot of people were promoted after the disaster.

Housed in private quarters and barns, and without any operation scheduled, we spent the turn of the year in Slovakia. At least it was a bit quieter for us. New Year's Eve was celebrated, not like in peacetime, but it was celebrated nonetheless. And there was also better food this time and something to drink. In early January 1945, we received 300 new replacement prisoners from Krakow. Around 35 of them came to my company, which was now 75 strong. I had the new guys line up and told them, "You may have heard that a large number of prisoners deserted to the Russians a week ago. If there is one among you who is planning to do the same, then I will shoot you myself. Do you understand?"

Training was then resumed with the new men. Marching and shooting theory, and now also training with the bazooka. For that there was an *Oberscharführer* with two men and about fifteen bazookas. Until then, I had only shot a bazooka twice in Warsaw. They explained the procedure: pull the locking pin, flip open the sight, and aim through the three sight notches (distance estimation required). To fire, position the weapon over the shoulder when prone, kneeling, and standing, or in the armpit when kneeling and standing. It was particularly important to point out that no one should be standing behind the barrel when firing; otherwise he could get burned by the jet of fire from the propellant. Tanks should actually be targeted between the turret and the track. But this was hardly easy to put into practice. Aiming was so imprecise that you either had to get up to a few meters close, or just roughly aim and pull the trigger. The projectile could probably fly close to 100 meters, but where it landed was pure chance. The best distance was up to about 40 meters. How it was supposed to work at longer distances was a mystery to me. Maybe the bazooka was useful in close combat, or in the forest, or in hilly areas. After around an hour of training on a somewhat remote field, we fired the fifteen bazookas. The target was a tree standing about forty meters away. From the fifteen shots fired, only one hit the tree, three landed close by, some scattered wide, and four or five didn't explode at all. On one of the bazookas, the propellant didn't even ignite. Anyway, my shot landed around two meters from the tree, and I was satisfied enough. But the men ridiculed this wonder weapon ever since, which was quite understandable.

The Battle for Lubisko and Guben

In early February, the move to Silesia was announced. Things must be pretty hot there, if they wanted us to go. We arrived in Guben by rail transport and were first led to a barracks where recruits of the *Großdeutschland* Division were housed. We stayed the night there, and by the next day we were already ordered to cross over the Neisse. While the first regiment was moved farther to the east on the Bober, we marched to the south toward Lubsko, which had been occupied by Ivan the previous evening. The mood was already depressing. Refugees were steadily streaming from the east – either on foot, by cart, or on trains. It was especially depressing on the trains, because there were just so many miserable people who had lost everything. It was enough to make you furious. Momm gathered the four company commanders and explained that the regiment was going to line up the next day with the armored infantry. Dirlewanger would personally command the operation and we would recapture Lubisko.

Our 2nd Battalion was deployed in the middle and pushed forward to the city center, supported by infantry fighting vehicles. The Russians were visibly surprised. They broke away quickly with little resistance, and we were even able to capture numerous prisoners, as well as weapons and equipment. Dirlewanger – who we had nicknamed "Gandhi" in 1940, due to his resemblance to the Indian statesman – was injured during the offensive. He had never been a coward, and when he was there during operations he was always at the front. In and around the town itself we found quite a few defiled women and girls, as well as executed elderly people. Around sixty dead French prisoners of war were also found lying at a brick factory. Why had the Russians killed them? Maybe they thought they were French volunteers of the Wehrmacht? The Frenchmen all still had their uniforms on.

First, we cleared Lubisko of scattered Red Army soldiers – they had probably slept through the retreat of their units or were distracted by the plundering. After we had seen the murdered German civilians, we didn't waste any more time here. We buried the dead soldiers and civilians, and tried to prepare defensive positions. By that night, the Red Army was already dropping heavy artillery fire on the city. Strangely enough, though, only a few houses were destroyed by it. The next day, Ivan attacked from the southeast with tanks. Because we received the order to pull back behind the Neisse, we were able to clear Lubisko again without much resistance. The armored infantry covered us with anti-tank canons and then drove back at full pelt. But Ivan was right at our heels. We reached the area ahead of Guben from a southwest direction, and were

Battle for Lubisko.

supposed to take up improvised positions immediately. I was appalled when I saw the young guys who were standing or lying in the trenches there. They were all probably sixteen or seventeen-year-old boys. Of course, I wasn't even twenty-five yet. We were briefed by a couple of Army members, and not a half an hour went by before we heard someone shout, "Look out, tanks!" We couldn't see them yet, but we heard them quietly rattling by. I said to my company troop leader, "Go and get as many bazookas as you can. Organize them somehow and turn them away from our guys quickly."

He hopped out of the trench and ran off. After about fifteen minutes, he was back again with six bazookas in his arms. Then we saw the enemy tanks approaching. Some were on the street, some on the left and right in the fields, then they stopped and fired. Behind us stood a camouflaged anti-tank cannon, which didn't fire back yet. We pushed ourselves deeper into the trenches. The tanks were probably still 300 or 400 meters away, and the bazookas were useless at this distance. It was sheer madness, actually. Around fifteen tanks were approaching us, and we only had a single anti-tank cannon. The tanks came closer and a few stopped again and fired, but the others kept driving, moving forward relentlessly.

Then there was a blast behind us; the anti-tank gun had started to shoot. They shot maybe three or four times, and then it was quitting time for some reason. The Russian tanks were getting closer and closer, and we stood in the trenches like deer in the headlights. A dispatch rider came racing up and yelled, "Order from the battalion: relocate to the edge of the city." I quickly pondered how we could accomplish this without being shot down in the open field. I couldn't come up with anything, so I simply commanded, "Move to the outskirts. Make sure that all weapons are brought along!" The men jumped out of the trenches, ran about 400 meters, and after a short breather in a gully, another 400 meters back to the edge of town. Luckily, we didn't lose anyone on this occasion.

Then we made it to the first houses in Gubens. There was a tense calm here, but I was reassured by the fact that there were better positions here along and between the rows of houses, and that heavy weaponry was available.

Now there were older soldiers, too. They were smoking cigarettes and looking at us sedately. I sent a dispatch rider away immediately in order to establish contact with Momm. The enemy tanks came closer and on the horizon I could already make out more units. When the first armor-piercing shells struck, the tank destroyers received their order to fire. In short succession, the 7.5 Pak shot at the nearing tanks and was able to score several hits. The Russian tanks farther away were also advancing at high speeds. Red Army soldiers were glued to them like flies. They turned in our direction, stopped, shot, and continued to come our way. Our Pak wasn't able to hold them back, and they continued to close in. We heard, "Change of position," and the Pak was dismantled and pulled back. We didn't really know where we should look: at the retreating tank destroyers, or ahead to the thundering tanks edging ever closer. The dispatch appeared again and shouted, "The positions are being moved farther back. We should take off." Meanwhile, the explosions were becoming more frequent and

Seventeen and eighteen-year old recruits of the armored infantry replacement and training regiment "Grossdeutschland" hold Guben until reinforcements arrive.

the tanks were already 400 meters away. We moved out. We ran back toward the city center and found cover behind makeshift barricades. Shortly after, the tanks reached the line we had just left.

The Pak took up new positions in the streets and immediately began to fire at the enemy tanks. When it made it to the first major streets there was an almost direct field of fire, and the Russian tanks, limited in their movement, were sitting ducks. But this changed when the enemy infantry arrived, too. Without hesitation they charged into the first houses and started shooting from the windows at everything that moved. The Pak operators also suffered losses when the Russians began to fire at them from the top floors. A dispatcher came running and yelled, "Counter attack. You have to get Ivan out of the houses." I went to my platoon leaders and ordered the men to storm the houses on both ends of the main road. I had a bad feeling about it. Not only were Russian tanks circling around here, but the fact that we had to go uncovered against an enemy who was holed up in houses was an unpleasant thought.

We ran off, armed with numerous hand grenades and bazookas, our hob-nailed boots clattering on the cobblestone streets – probably more useful in the countryside, since we lacked a secure grip on the cobblestone. Shortly after, we emerged from behind the street barricades, the first Russian sub-machine gun salvos pounded the house walls and the street we were running on. One or two men were hit and fell over. No stopping – keep on running. Each group ran into a house entrance, and the Karabiner proved once again to be a poor modern weapon. The Russians, who were mostly equipped with sub-machine guns, were far superior. Among us, only those in charge (company, platoon, and squad leaders) had sub-machine guns or assault rifles.

Into the houses and quickly into the apartments – hand grenades in and continue on. Ivan was usually on the first or second floor. Strangely enough, there were fewer and fewer the higher we went. Were they afraid to go up there? Most of them came from poor villages and had never been this close to civilization. The results varied greatly. One group was able to win over a house; one got stuck on the ground floor and another on a higher floor. So far, the counter attack was not successful. From maybe six houses, two were in our hands, two in Russian hands, and two were still being contested. So we sent men over for backup. Two more houses were taken, and then it was over. Thus, the mission hadn't been completely executed. I quickly thought about firing off a couple of bazookas at the opposing houses when a man in my company noticed two T-34s rolling up. They immediately began shooting at us. The window crossbars blew out, the plaster crumbled, and in addition to the incredible amount of dust, a fire broke out.

Shooting Down a Tank

"Duck down and get away from the window. Think." First and foremost, the damned tanks have to be taken care of. I said to both of my dispatchers, "Let's Go. Each of you grab two bazookas and follow me." We stumbled down the wooden stairway from the second floor and ran up to the windows of the ground floor, where the men of my company stood. Both tanks stood to our right, staggered on the street, and took turns shooting in the houses. From this angle we could see alright, but aiming and shooting with the bazookas was impossible. Going out to the street was suicide. For the time being, we had to just take cover and wait. Then suddenly, the engines roared, the tracks rattled, and one of the tanks started to move forward. He proceeded reluctantly, and then stopped after a few meters. It was just enough time for me to take aim at him. I had one of my dispatchers move away from behind me and watch the windows across the way, so that none of the Russians could pick me off. I gave the other one my sub-machine gun so that he could shoot at any tank crew that may climb out.

I released the safety on the bazooka, flipped the sight up, aimed at the tank – it may have been 30 meters away – and pushed the lever down. The grenade left a trail of smoke, hit the tank, and there, before my strained eyes, was an explosion, and then a heavy emission of smoke. I quickly ducked for cover before peeking through the empty window once again. The thing was still standing there smoking – nothing was moving. I had shot down a Russian tank. That was in the afternoon of February 22, 1945.

In the meantime, it was already getting slightly dark. Suddenly, around thirty Russians emerged from behind the shot-down tank and ran by us to the other side of the street. What was going on? In that instant it was "open fire," and they fled into the house, where their comrades were still waiting. The situation was getting more and more uncomfortable for us. I called my platoon leaders over and told them that I planned to storm both houses across the street as soon as it was dark enough. The darkness was of little advantage, though, since the street was quite illuminated by the glow of the fire from the surrounding houses. Nevertheless, at around 7 p.m., I had a platoon line up at each house. Incredibly, there was little defensive fire on the street. Instead, heavy gun battles took place in the houses and apartments. I stayed with the company troops and some others on the other street front and provided cover fire. After around fifteen minutes, a man signaled from the house on the left that everything was okay. I then pointed to the neighboring house. He understood, and

(TOP) A T34 SHOT DOWN IN GUBEN.
(BOTTOM) ENGAGED IN URBAN COMBAT.

shortly thereafter a few men ran to the apartment house on the right, which was also quickly cleared.

It took a few hours, but our mission was finally fulfilled. I sent a dispatch rider to Momm. After about 40 minutes, he came back and said that we should pull back; Ivan had already pushed through Guben to the Neisse on other streets. We only had a limited amount of space in front of us, so I gave the order to retreat. A downed T-34 notwithstanding, the entire action cost our side five dead and 12 wounded from around 60 men. We moved back in the flickering glow of the burning houses. There were no longer any people at the spot where we had run forward from behind the barricades around midday. Lying there were only the cartridges from the Pak, shell casings, and various pieces of equipment. The dispatcher went ahead, and in 20 minutes we made it to the new HKL in Guben.

I reported to *Hauptsturmführer* Momm, who had set up his command post in a basement, where there was still even preserved fruit on the shelves.

The battalion staff was made up almost entirely of demoted Wehrmacht officers. Momm was very busy, and briefly bent over to glance at a city map, while I delivered my report of occupying houses and shooting down the tank, as well as the planned retreat. He raised his eyebrows and said, "The battle commander is done here. He's completely overextended. He probably wants to spare his kids." By that he meant the sixteen and seventeen-year-old recruits of the Armored Infantry Replacement and Training Regiment "Großdeutschland" and their regiment commander, who was appointed local commander. Major Theermann was ordered by Hitler to defend Guben as a bridgehead. He shot himself after he had been threatened with court martial when he wouldn't defend Guben to the last man. Hitler probably planned to line up a counter offensive from here. Colonel Berger became the new battle commander, and he immediately issued numerous new orders. The troops already considered the crossing of the Neisse, in the western section of Guben, as an impossible distance. A few times we also saw soldiers dangling from trees. They were probably deserters and wore signs around their necks that read, "I'm a coward" or "I'm betraying German women and children."

Momm showed me a small section on the map and sent me there with around eight men. I look back now and think that it had to have been very difficult, because this important bridgehead of Guben was only defended by a local militia, old *Landesschützen*, young children, and a motley crowd of others. Back then, though, I didn't think too much about it. We fought for about three weeks in the almost completely destroyed old town. Streets repeatedly changed hands. In one house there would be Russians, in the other house Germans. Supported by rabble-rousers, counterattacks were continually carried out and Guben would be recaptured momentarily. Then the Russians would attack with tanks again at night and the "reconquest" would be over. We suffered heavy losses due to the constant action. When we were finally relieved in early March 1945 and allowed to cross the Neisse to the west, I had 25 men left from the initial 75 men and the replacements inserted during the operation.

Members of the *SS-Sturmbrigade* "Dirlewanger" during the battle at Guben.

We were then moved to the SS training facility Kurmark, and we stayed at the empty "Lieberose" work camp near Jamlitz. Jews had once been detained in this former work camp, and were probably moved to Sachsenhausen. While the squads were quartered in the wooden barracks, those of us in charge used the accommodations of the guard battalion, which had moved away to the front.

Some new probation troops had already arrived; some arrived in the following days. They were Wehrmacht felons, around 2,000 of them, along with several hundred concentration camp prisoners. Around 400 court-martialed SS members also came from a SS probation unit in Bohemia. The *SS Sturmbrigade* "Dirlewanger" was at full strength again.

The squads, platoons, and companies were put together and training began. In addition to the prisoners, members of the Navy and the Air Force, who still had to be trained in infantry combat, were also there. Of course, it wasn't proper training. In fact, our primary objective was to try to straighten things out. The situation was almost catastrophic. We were trying to set up a unit within ten days that was even supposed to represent a division supported by other Army troops. We didn't know any of these guys. Leaders were assigned to groups and no one knew how each man would do. Can we rely on this guy or will it be a fiasco? As much as possible, these positions were also handed over to men who had been with us for around one or two years, or men who were former guard personnel with the probation troops and had been assigned to us. They were usually older guys, too. Maybe they had been good in the Wehrmacht prisons, but they weren't prepared for action on the front lines. Some former commanders and junior command officers who had been demoted were also used. On the whole, it was hardly a useful bunch and their varicolored uniforms painted a hodgepodge picture.

A lot of paperwork had to be taken care of. Pay books were collected and some had to be re-issued. They were provided to the new unit like the service books. Reports had to be written to the military district command – unbelievable bureaucracy just six weeks before the war's end. I took a look at the personnel paperwork of the Wehrmacht convicts. Main offenses included: unauthorized absence from troop, desertion, theft, assault, and insubordination. These were all people whose reliability really had be questioned. To my surprise, I remained company commander, even though there were so many demoted commanders and junior officers available. Momm had really put his trust in me. Then, one day, I was ordered to see the *Hauptsturmführer*, who quickly said, "Here, congratulations," and handed me a tank destroyer stripe. "Go to the Sergeant and have the badge entered into your pay book." The day began in the work camp around 5:45 a.m., and ended at 7:30 p.m. In between, it was mainly organizational things, training, and very bad food. There was pretty much only flat water soup with sugar beet pulp in it. I also remember several cases when the punishment of repeatedly disobedient probation troops would be announced in the battalion or regiment command. Sometimes a drum head court martial could also convene, and then someone would be shot.

GUBEN IN FLAMES.

After curfew for the probation troops, there were always a few lead officers gathered at the barrack lounges. We drank and ate something, and talked about this and that. I always sat there with three or four men who I had known since 1940/41. Just before we were supposed to march off to the front lines again, one of them said, "With these bastards, we're all going down!" Everyone agreed, and even I had the feeling that there was no happy ending waiting. "The Russians will be here in four weeks at the latest, and then in eight weeks the party will be over – if we even get to see the end." There was definitely some truth to this. Who wanted to kick the bucket at five 'til midnight? On top of that, no one knew how the probation troops would conduct themselves. Our regiment commander, Ehlers, was strung up in the forest in pieces by former prisoners at the end of April 1945. "Maybe we should think about how we can get out of this before it's too late!"

It was dangerous to be talking like this, because it was just an invitation for the troops to go AWOL. I ended the conversation by saying that I was going to bed. But actually I lay in bed and ran through the situation in my head. How could I disappear as a company commander, and where would I go? The next day I looked for the guy who initiated this and asked him, "What did you mean yesterday? Have you already thought about it?" He answered that he had been thinking about it for a while, but also didn't know how he could pull it off.

A few days later, we were put on standby and the move to the front lines began. We went part of the way by train and part of the way on foot or by truck through Cottbus to Forst. First, we dug out positions in a second line, and then took over the first line from a Wehrmacht unit, directly on the Neisse. The mood was depressed and I felt overburdened as company commander. In emergency situations, people usually rise to the occasion, but now that we were lying quietly on the front, I noticed that I no longer knew how to relate to others psychologically, especially under difficult circumstances like this. I was nothing more than a young lad, almost 25-years-old, who had had no better schooling or any kind of training.

Along the Neisse, trenches had been dug out and wooden bunkers were set up in the ground. The Russians were completely calm; it seemed that the war was already over. Looking through binoculars to the eastern banks, Ivan was going about his normal daily routine. It was so calm that the order came to resume training the probation troops. Momm was very concerned and we company commanders had to meet with him often. We were to report if any one of us noticed defeatism spreading. One day Weisse, who had become First General Staff Officer, also arrived. He drove in a bucket car to the individual battalions and companies, and wanted to get a feel for the morale. Since fall 1944, he had worn the German Cross in gold and he left a very rigid impression, as he had before. He came by our position too, and after my report he asked how the men were doing. I couldn't really say much to that because I had only known these guys for about three weeks. "If anything happens, crack down immediately by any means necessary!" he said in a Saxon dialect, and climbed back into his bucket car. That was the last time I saw Weisse. He survived the war, joined the Gehlen Organization, and then got paid by the USA (CIA). They probably weren't interested in what kind of pig Weisse was, or if he was a war criminal. Interestingly, he was considered missing in 1963, the same year I was questioned by criminal investigators. Surely the files regarding his activities for the BND are available.

Around April 21st, when the Russians succeeded in combining troops penetrating from the north and the south, we were surrounded with around 70,000 men. The next day, the Russians gained a foothold over the Neisse, north of our positions near Groß Breesen. In order to support the weak forces there – they were mainly police units – our battalion (now called the 2nd Waffen Grenadier Regiment of the SS 73) was withdrawn and shuttled by truck through Guben, to the north. Thus, we were taken out of the framework of our former brigade (or new division), and never went back to it. In rainy weather, we were instructed to line up on the southwestern bridgehead. There were no positions available here. In fact, the policemen were lying across from the enemy in quickly thrown together foxholes, and apparently they were under orders to establish a bridgehead first. They wouldn't have been able to withstand any resistance. Now they were lying, sitting, or standing in the damp holes, and were happy that backup had arrived.

By the next day, however, the order came for the entire section to withdraw. We packed up our things again and pulled back. In addition to the police, the men of the SS Guard Battalion "Kurmark" marched with us toward Lieberose, which we had marched away from four weeks ago on our way to the front. There were a few geezers on hand again. Next to old men in their 50s, there were also a lot of younger ethnic Germans who, based on their physiognomy, had to be counted among the prisoners rather than guards. The retreat through Lieberose Heide created a greater loss of solidarity among the troops than the advancing Russians did. I can't recall any real battles. In truth, we just kept marching to the west and were shot at once in a while by enemy airplanes. The Russian ground troops just moved ahead without attacking us. Whether that was because we didn't fall into their main attack strip or because Ivan didn't want to lose any more men, I don't know. It was clear that it would come to an end in the next ten to fourteen days. The hope that many had was that an alliance would be formed with the Americans and collectively a front to the east would be established. We held on to this straw of hope when Roosevelt died, but it was only window dressing and I wasn't holding my breath.

When we made it to the "Kurmark" military training area, positions were taken and the advancing Russians were even shot at for a short time. They stopped immediately and didn't proceed until we broke down again. Because the northern front was burning, the order was issued to march together with the police battalion – I think it even involved a field replacement battalion – and the guard battalion in a northwest direction via Groß Leuthen to Wolzig. On the way, the smaller farmsteads and villages were all cleaned out. We went into the houses and searched for food. In some of the cellars there were stores of potatoes, pickles, and apples, which we greedily ate. The food was a catastrophe. There was almost nothing left. Once in a while the

Sergeant was able to organize some bread. The morale among the probation troops was divided: some walked lethargically in the columns, others were "complainers" or even Communists who were happy. I didn't care. On one hand, I knew the end was near anyway; on the other hand, I didn't want to catch a stray bullet. So we marched in the direction that was given to us.

Near Wolzig, a meeting of company commanders took place. The battalion headquarters was in a small house; in the living room an orderly was giving out real coffee. I was surprised. Where did it come from? Surely it was found in a house somewhere. It smelled wonderful. Momm announced that we were now under command of the XI SS Army Corps and should expect to see some action soon. Since it involved a key point in the battle, he wanted to prevent the battalion from seeing heavy action. In Hungary, he had seen for himself what could happen. He said that he wanted to drive to the commanding general and that I should come with him, because I had experienced the battle near Ipolysag for myself. Together with his adjutants and a driver, we went by truck to the command post of the Corps. He was staying at an estate, and it was all hustle and bustle there. Momm reported his presence and we were told to wait in the hallway. We waited for almost an hour and a half, then we were called into a large room where several maps lay on tables pushed together. Newsmen sat at switchboards and radio installations along the walls. *Obergruppenführer* (Senior Group Leader) Kleinheisterkamp stood at the table. *Hauptsturmführer* Momm went to him, saluted, and reported that his battalion would be called into action, but it was made up of prisoners released from concentration camps four weeks ago and court-martialed soldiers, many of whom were communists and deserters. Deployment would be irresponsible and would inevitably lead to a fiasco. The unit had already experienced this four months ago in Hungary, when over 600 men deserted to the Red Army. Kleinheisterkamp, who seemed very unsteady, tired, and lethargic, but also hard and disciplined, answered that every man would be needed here, because if the Russians could break through the encircled area now, it would be all over. Momm replied that he was clear, but he wanted to inform the Commanding General about the events in Hungary. Deploying his battalion was a danger for the entire front line. Kleinheisterkamp spoke with his First General Staff Officer and told us to wait outside. We waited for about twenty minutes. Then he came to us and said, "the orders have been changed." The battalion should move to the south and try to meet up with its own division again.

Halbe

Since we didn't have any communication lines to the division, and we didn't know exactly where our troops were, this only seemed to be a mission to get us as far away as possible. Maybe they were afraid that 600 men would suddenly get out of control? For the time being, we marched toward Klein Köris, alongside an increasing army of civilians with little handcarts and trailers. Reports came in sporadically that there were attempts to break through to the west over the Reichsautobahn, for example. The mood was awful. We weren't in battle, but the situation was catastrophic all the same. The civilians – elderly people and women with small children – who staggered with us to the south and southwest over forest pathways appeared desolate and hopeless. We rested in the forests, and maybe this is how Richard Wagner had imagined the *Götterdämmerung* (Twilight of the Gods). Marching single file, we reached the village of Halbe. Just before town, we could already see numerous dead soldiers and civilians lying in the forests. At the entrance and the area around the train station, the dead were actually lying around in piles. There were also dead Red Army soldiers. We didn't really pay attention to this; instead, we pushed into the village like a herd. It was full of dead bodies. A huge battle must have taken place here. Since Russians and Germans alike had been killed in great numbers, the village probably switched hands several times. The doors of homes stood open and we could also see the dead lying inside. Everything was just strewn all over the streets: burned out cars, weapons, and equipment, strollers and puppets, everything.

I wondered if any of this made sense at all. Maybe it would be better to attempt to break through in small groups in another area. But somehow we just kept walking *en masse* and hoped that we got through. No one wanted to be in a Russian prisoner of war camp. Concentrating only on the few meters around me, I lost sight of my company, and honestly, I didn't really care. In truth, I was thinking about what I would do when I made it out of the cauldron. I didn't look to my left or right anymore, I just kept walking, wedged in a crowd that kept pushing forward. I thought of the pictures depicting how the Stone Age people probably drove their prey over a cliff. The village ended, and not far off was the autobahn. Hopefully, freedom was waiting on the other side. Suddenly, heavy artillery fire began to hit the area and there were countless casualties. But no one paid attention anymore to who fell injured. They were probably trampled to death. No one cared anymore.

THE RETREAT THROUGH HALBE TO THE 12TH ARMY.

Running at full speed, we crossed the autobahn and made it to another forested area. There were artillery explosions there, too, and casualties. I was lucky! I just kept running. Two older field gendarmes stood at a small crossing and announced the route of march. All around them was a cluster of soldiers and civilians who wanted to find out what was going on. As I was walking past, I heard that Russians were still everywhere to the north and south. Our own troops from the 12th Army were planning to strike against them from the west, but they were still around 50 km away. Fifty kilometers! There was no time to waste. We had to keep going as fast as possible. The farther away we could get the better. There were only around ten men from my company marching with me now. The rest had either intentionally or unintentionally lost touch. I really didn't mind. I hoped that I wouldn't be held responsible for it and, if so, I would just blame everything on the mess we were in.

While we were pressing forward on forest trails, I wondered how things were playing out. Was the war over? What was with the Americans? Did they join us to fight the Russians? As I was pondering, I finally noticed the suddenly irruptive battle noise. The Russians had set up a blockade of rip-booms and tanks and brought the columns to a halt. The noise was intense. The head of the column lined up immediately to break through, with the last infantry fighting vehicles and tanks. We were so far back that we noticed, even though we didn't see it. I asked my last few soldiers to follow me and we pushed on. We tried to gain ground, at times even running at a quick pace. More and more bodies of those killed in action were lying on the forest floor. Intuitively, I decided that if we were to break through, then it would have to be at the front near the tanks, not in the back with the civilians and the often-apathetic soldiers.

Privates lined up to attack and secured the area to the left and right of the road. After that, the column began to move again and the people – old and young civilians and soldiers – hobbled on toward the west. No rest, no time to waste. How did it go in the *Cornet*? "Ride, ride, ride, through the day and through the night!" And we ran and ran and ran. Eventually, there was a wide flat that we had to get over. Russian planes circled above and shot at us. I kicked it into high gear and ran with all my might. Next to me, behind me, and in front of me, people were falling in a hail of bullets – I was lucky, as I was so often before, and made it to the German lines. There was a division of RAD members here in improvised positions. These sixteen and seventeen-year-old boys still had their RAD uniforms on. They were lying there with a steel helmet on their heads and a machine gun in a firing position, and they looked at us with big eyes.

The Last Days of the War and Returning Home

I wanted to say, "Piss off kids, there's too much heat here." But I didn't say anything. Instead, I went further back, where the field gendarme and some officers from the division were directing the arriving groups. While the mass was sent farther back – a shuttle was arranged for the wounded and the worn out – my remaining people and I were sent to a combat group, which was to support the RAD kids on the seam to the neighboring corps. Then we were loaded into vehicles and moved to the southwest, near Coswig.

The young guys were probably relieved when we backed them up. Some of us moved to improvised foxholes directly on the front, while others went to the staggered second line in the back. American troops were said to be southwest of us, and the Russians were southeast. By the next evening already, we broke down and moved north during the night. My buddy, who at the "Kurmark" SS military training area a short while ago had brought up the topic of leaving the troops, came up to me and said, "Hey, if we aren't quick about it now, maybe Ivan will arrest us by tomorrow. We should try to get over the Elbe tonight. Then we'll definitely be captured by the Americans first. Maybe we'll even get to go home."

In light of the situation, I agreed. What did we have to lose? I definitely didn't want to fall into the hands of the Russians, and who knew how the delayed retreat would shape up in the next few days. Without further ado, we used the darkness, the confusion of the nighttime relocation, and the fact that no one paid attention to others in our combat group, and walked carefully in a southern direction. We went through a kind of no man's land. The Americans had stopped on the Mulde and waited there for the advance of the Red Army, which was taking its time. This was our chance. We crossed the Elbe at the grand Wörlitzer Park and hurriedly ran on. Unfortunately, our departure had been so spontaneous that we hadn't prepared at all for it. We only brought what we had at our position – nothing to drink and very little to eat.

Nevertheless, we ran at a brisk pace all night long and, after a short break, we continued early the next morning. Then we paused for a moment and observed the area around us. Were there possibly other troops here? Or the Americans? Or the Russians? What should we do with our uniforms? Until we knew for sure that the war was over, we wanted to keep them on. You never knew whether you would by chance run into a German unit, and then at least we could explain ourselves as scattered troops. We ran through the Dübener Heide and got something to eat and drink from the terrified people. They were expecting the Russians any day. "What are the Russians like?" we were asked. What were we supposed to say? I didn't know how the Russians would act towards German civilians – but if they acted like we did in Russia, then I suspected it wouldn't be good!

We discussed what we wanted to do next. My home was about 500 km away. By foot, and probably only at night, that would be about a 14-day march. I couldn't envision that working out. My buddy, a former prisoner from Buchenwald, was from the Harz, and said, "Come on, let's march to my hometown. My family is there and they'll help us. You can stay as long as you like, and then we'll see how you will get home." It was a good suggestion – mainly because the locals had already warned us that the American troops were in the surrounding area. We arranged some civilian clothing and threw our uniforms into a pit. I took my pay book and detached the decorations from my field blouse. Somehow I wanted to be able to identify myself if necessary. And the decorations? They were supposed to be a sort of memento. Then we turned to the west and, at night, we swam across the Mulde. The bridges were all guarded by U.S. troops, with brisk vehicle traffic back and forth.

To my buddy's place near Mansfeld it was around 100 km. We could probably make it in a maximum of four days (nights). It was manageable. At night we scampered along, like so many other soldiers apparently, from village to village and through forests and fields to the Harz. We continually encountered individuals or small groups that also had set out on their own. We didn't talk much. We always tried to cover as much ground as possible at night. And we were actually lucky that we didn't fall into the hands of the Americans, because we couldn't see anything. We didn't know whether there were any guard posts out there somewhere. We were very lucky and actually made it to a little town near Mansfeld after three nights. In the morning, my buddy walked over to a house and knocked. After a short time the door opened, and he disappeared into the house. Thank God he was taken in. I waited and waited. After about twenty minutes, a little boy came running up to me and brought me inside, too.

His uncle, aunt, and grandmother were standing there in the kitchen, and he talked on and on. "Well, my boy, at least you're back now," said grandma, and his uncle asked, "And what's your plan now? Surely you guys have to report somewhere." "Never again," his wife said. "Be happy that he made it back in one piece!" Needless to say, these people were overwhelmed with our unannounced visit. I didn't feel very comfortable there. "I'll go to your mother's now and bring her here," said the aunt, and disappeared. The mood slowly loosened up a bit. "Do you fellows want to wash up?" the grandmother asked, as she hobbled around in the kitchen. A few minutes later, there was hot nettle tea and everyone had a thick piece of bread and a sausage in their hand. Then the aunt arrived back with her sister. It was a moment of great joy. It had been a good decision after all.

We decided to hide ourselves for the time being, until the end of the war was official. Two days later, the radio announced the unconditional capitulation. A big sigh of relief – now the horror was finally over. It wouldn't get any worse. Now I had to figure out how to get home. The uncle said, "Well, you need some kind of papers. Otherwise the Americans will snatch you up straight away."

The next day, a former concentration camp prisoner came to town, still dressed in his blue and white striped prisoner uniform. "Hey, I know him!" said my buddy. "I'll go and get his clothes for you. Then maybe you can return home as a prisoner. They probably aren't controlled by the Americans." Said and done. That evening, he disappeared and came back about three hours later. Not only did he have the clothes, but he also returned triumphantly with a document that had been issued by the Americans. What it said, we didn't know – it was either a certificate proving that the bearer of this document was free of infectious diseases or it was a release from the Sachsenhausen concentration camp. In any case, it listed the name of the prisoner, together with the prisoner number, as well as the designation of the concentration camp. It was genius. I wanted to stay one more day and then try to get home again by train.

I received best wishes and something to eat and drink. Then I marched off to Eisleben, around 10 km away, with a backpack containing civilian clothes, among other things. Some of the people who saw me in my striped uniform looked at me with sympathy, but most gave me a deprecating look. Access to the train station was no problem. There were Americans standing there – some of them were checking papers, while others just casually smoked cigarettes or chewed gum. I inquired about how I could get home. I got the information in a not-so-friendly manner that I should first go to Halle. I could change trains there to Naumburg, and from there to Regensburg via Nuremberg. I didn't need a ticket for it. Just try to find a seat.

The train stations were all teeming with people. The Red Cross was handing out tea. There were soldiers who wanted to get home like me, but were stopped by the Americans and brought to detention centers. I had it better. I was checked by the Americans once – one guy even gave me three cigarettes – and on I went. "You came from prison?" someone asked me in a train compartment. "Yeah, I was in Sachsenhausen." "How did you end up there?" "I had a problem with an SA man at the gendarmerie." This was pretty much the truth. Deploring head-nodding, and then looking silently out of the window again. In the bombed cities, there was only desolation. Waiting in the destroyed train stations for connecting trains. Sleeping overnight in the waiting hall. Tea and bread from the Red Cross – cookies from the Americans. Departure chaos. Running to the next train in the morning. Delay. Waiting on the platform. Watching the people hurrying by and waiting. What did they have planned? Then the train arrives two hours late. People are hanging on it like grapes. Unbelievable scramble, pushing and shoving. The train sits and sits – then finally it begins to move. It's going to Regensburg. I'm making progress, and now I wonder what the future holds. First to the farmer, and hopefully I can get work again and have a permanent place to stay. Regensburg train station. I get off, get my bearings. So much destruction – supposedly, we were still fighting against the Americans here. Through the checkpoint, and walk to my hometown 10 km away. It took a while, though, because there were several checkpoints to cross in Regensburg. "My" American document was a clearance certificate. I got through everywhere.

The closer I got to my home, the less comfortable I felt in the prison clothes. A half a year ago I had come here as a "proud" *SS Oberscharführer* with a chest full of medals, and now I was a ragged prisoner. I wondered how I should proceed. Surely at some point I would have to report to the authorities and get my ration cards too, even though I didn't necessarily need them, because I could get food at the farm. But how should I report? As a former prisoner, or a deserted *SS Oberscharführer*? I didn't have any discharge papers in my name. Once outside of Regensburg, I disappeared into the forest and put my civilian clothes on. I put the prison clothes in my backpack, just in case. I continued on my way, and after around three hours I entered the farm. Everything looked dismal here too, as before – nothing had visibly changed since October 1944.

"Where did you come from?" the farmer asked me flatly. "Were you fighting in the area?" "No, south of Berlin, but I came back by train to Regensburg." "It was that easy? And you're in civilian clothes?" "Well, I was a little lucky." "Alright, I can't pay you, but you can sleep and eat here. Go to the foreman later and have him give you some work." It all went off without any problems. My mother came later and started to cry immediately, "Thank God that you're back again, my boy!"

War Captivity

It was already more difficult with the foreman. He looked even more haggard than before and let his complete disdain for me be known. But he gave me work and that was important. One day, when I had to go to the nearest big town, I was checked by U.S. soldiers. Since I didn't have any papers on me, they quickly took me with them. At the former gendarmerie I was questioned by a German-speaking officer. He wanted to know if I had been a soldier, and if I had served with the Wehrmacht, the police, or Waffen-SS. Then they wanted to see my pay book or my discharge papers. I couldn't produce any of it, and so they held me there for the time being. I stayed the night in a cell, together with two other men, and then we were brought to Regensburg. I ended up in a different camp than they did, however. It turned out that it was predominantly members of the Waffen-SS staying there. We didn't do anything in the camp. We snoozed and got bored. There was also almost nothing to eat.

After some time, a commission came to interrogate us. I told my story quite truthfully. I went to prison for poaching, and then had the opportunity to get out if I volunteered for service. First, I was in Poland for a year, and then two years in Belarus. And I had fought against the partisans. Obviously I didn't mention anything about our activities involving the civilian population. Because the *Sonderkommando* was unknown and had never fought against the Americans, I was dismissed from the interrogation relatively quickly. Others came out with bloody faces. Again, I was lucky.

In the fall of 1945, I went to an internment camp in Nuremberg-Langwasser. Here too – near the former site of the Nuremberg Rally – it was almost entirely members of the Waffen-SS. Unlike Regensburg, we had to reside in holes in the ground at first. There was practically no hygiene. Later, we were taken on work assignments and we stayed in factory halls. We were primarily assigned with cleaning up the rubble in Nuremberg. Occasionally, we were interrogated individually. We stood in front of one or two desks, behind which one to three interrogators sat. There were usually two others standing or leaning somewhere in the room. Everything was mixed – women were also among them. The interrogators often spoke relatively good German. They could have been immigrants. They continually asked questions about the unit and the operations. Interestingly enough, sometimes the questions were very specific. They wanted to know where we had been on such and such day, whether cooperation with Ivan existed, or whether there had possibly been any incidents involving Allied troops, and they wanted to find out if we were involved in any way.

Little by little, barracks were built and the camp was improved with a camp chapel and a theater. We were also able to take classes – English courses, for example. Parolees were constantly being released into the world; we were supposed to be shipped off to Russia or France. In April 1946, there was an act of vengeance by a Jewish underground organization. The bread that we had received every day was poisoned with arsenic. But nobody died, because the Americans granted us proper medical assistance right away – some GIs had also eaten the bread and were poisoned. In addition to severe stomach cramps, some lost hair or teeth. I too had serious stomach pain, and landed in an American hospital. I felt better after a few days. But I also had to say goodbye to a few of my teeth.

Postwar Period

I don't know whether it was a consequence of the attempted poisoning or not, but when I recovered, I was released with the others. It was almost one year to the day after my so-called "Automatic Arrest." I was now 26 years old and I was lucky once again. A lot of those who fell into Russian hands didn't come home until 1955 or even 1956.

I took the train from Nuremberg to Regensburg and then wandered happily home again. Now I had an official discharge paper and was able to handle the one checkpoint easily. I registered at all of the local authorities and then began to work on the farm again. But because I wasn't satisfied with it anymore, I started to work for the Americans in a metalworking shop in Regensurg. I was also able to get an American driver's license for passenger cars and commercial trucks. In 1948, my working relationship with the Americans ended (I was denazified for 50 Marks), and I became a driver for a trucking company in Regensburg. At first, I drove a truck carrying building materials in between Nuremberg, Weiden, Passau and Augsburg. Then it became too messy for me, and I applied at a passenger transport company. The owner paid for the necessary driver's license and, starting in 1952, I drove school buses. I got along well with my boss. When he later expanded his business to include bus tours, I drove regularly to Austria, Italy, and Switzerland. I liked it a lot. That's what I did until I retired in 1985.

Four years later came the fall of the Berlin Wall and German reunification. Who would have thought? The Soviet Union collapsed too, but peace didn't last in Europe, or the rest of the world. The hunger for power and the economic interests of individuals and organizations continues to lead to war, and it will probably go on like this forever.

Looking Back At My Time as a Soldier

At 85 years of age, I sat down to record my memories on paper. I don't think they are special by any means. Every person has their own individual experiences. Everyone has good and bad luck in life; some more than others. I was often lucky. Why? I don't know.

I wrote down my story in order to show others what humans are capable of. We humans think too little, and we are not courageous enough. That's the way it is unfortunately and I'm no exception. I was never a member of the NSDAP, and I never belonged to the German Youth or the Hitler Youth. My first contact was the obligatory *Reichsarbeitsdienst* (RAD, Reich Labor Service), which was actually fun for me back then. If I hadn't shot that stupid deer in the forest and gone to prison, I never would have considered joining the SS or Waffen-SS. Like most boys then, I would have preferred to become a U-boat driver, a fighter pilot, or a tank driver. But that didn't happen and I went to a unit that was given orders that were criminal.

Without thinking about it first, I carried out these orders – they came from my superiors. Today, I think that a country that appoints such people of authority and gives these kinds of orders is a criminal one. I first began to think about it when I was in Minsk, where I encountered Jews from Germany whom I didn't consider enemies, but rather fellow Germans, and when I was repeatedly ordered to clean out entire regions. Prior to that, I saw myself at war against the partisans because we were being shot at. Burning down villages that hadn't attacked us weighed on my conscience back then already.

I think it was 1958, when a man from Munich attempted to found a club of former members of the *Sonderkommando* "Dirlewanger." He was a former concentration camp prisoner who was locked up in Dachau as either a career criminal or a social misfit. Even I was informed about it through certain circles. Well, I was warned about the guy anyway. There were also plenty of scoundrels who swindled old war buddies for money long after the war.

In 1963, I was repeatedly interrogated by criminal investigators about my time with Dirlewanger. There were some legal proceedings against members of the *Sonderkommando* – mainly due to the Warsaw operation. Why did this take place twenty years after the fact? I gave my statements, but remained unaffected by the proceedings. Dirlewanger was the one among us all who did nothing wrong. He was precise and actually acted like a father and a confidant. He addressed us informally, and when we met him personally during operations, he often shared his chocolate or a sip from his canteen. A lot of his notoriety probably came after the war through the media, which always wants to write something sensational. They probably got their information from former members who had come to Dirlewanger as Wehrmacht deserters or social misfits and didn't have a nice life there.

Of course, that doesn't absolve Dirlewanger from his responsibility to have ordered so many crimes. Here he was ice cold. He received an order and he executed it. It didn't matter if it was liquidating civilians or a combat mission. He wasn't a coward. I think he was wounded over ten times in both world wars. He wore the golden Wound Badge, anyway.

How do I see my blame? I carried out orders that I myself consider criminal. Whether we could have refused to do it, is difficult to answer. My former company commander, Gast, told me that I wouldn't need to take part in the operations anymore if I had found a replacement. Weisse, in contrast, repeatedly had members of his commando shot for refusing to take orders, or for cowardice before the enemy. It's awful what we Germans did in the occupied areas, and it's difficult for me to relive those memories again.

Maybe my story will contribute to more responsible actions by legislative and executive powers. That would be my wish. A country is obligated to guide people in the right direction and develop responsible citizens. Many people can't do it alone. What did Goethe write? "Man should be noble, helpful and good!"

Appendix

Formation of the SS-Sonderkommando Dirlewanger

"The *Sonderkommando* Dirlewanger owes its creation to a 1940 order from Adolf Hitler, during the campaign in the west. One day, Himmler called me and told me that Hitler had ordered all men previously convicted of poaching with a weapon and those presently sitting in prison to be gathered up and recruited into a special commando. That Hitler even conceived such an utterly outrageous idea can be ascribed to the following reasons:

1.) He disliked hunting himself, and had only scorn and mockery for all hunters. Wherever he could provoke or ridicule a hunter, that's what he did.

2.) A woman had written him a letter around this time. The husband of this woman was a so-called 'old party member' and shot his deer in a state-owned forest. He was caught in the act and sentenced to two years in jail. The woman complained that her husband was sitting in prison, instead of being able to prove himself on the front lines."

When asked by his defender, Froschmann, about the creation of the *SS-Sturmbrigade* Dirlewanger during the Ministries Trial on June 2, 1948, the former chief of the SS Head Office, SS *Obergruppenfuhrer* Gottlob Berger, answered, "I wasn't happy about the order at the time..."[1]

This doesn't entirely coincide to the actual facts, though. In the end, it was Berger who had proposed Dirlewanger's release from the Wehrmacht and charged him with leading these men. The idea probably didn't come from Hitler either, but rather from Himmler. The *Reichsführer-SS* had a particular interest in researching Teutonism, and King Heinrich I was a significant figure.[2] He pardoned thieves and bandits if they would serve under him and ambush his enemies from then on. Himmler borrowed this, and presented his ideas to Hitler. On March 29, 1940, the *Reichsführer-SS* wrote the Reich's Minister of Justice, Dr. Gürtner:

The Führer has mandated that all poachers, particularly those of Bavarian and Austrian origin, who have violated the law by hunting with a gun, not with snares, can be freed from completing their sentences and granted amnesty with proper conduct by serving in special SS-affiliated riflemen companies for the duration of the war.

In its function as head of the German Police, the *Reichsführer-SS* reached an agreement with the *Reichsjägermeister* to enlist people to military service who were suspected of poaching, on the basis of the emergency military service act from October 15, 1938 (RGBl. I, pp. 1441). In order to differentiate these men from other criminals, only those who had been convicted exclusively of poaching with a gun should get the chance at rehabilitation on the front. Those who poached with snares or traps and those who had also committed other offenses, such as burglary or assault, for example, were excluded from it. Since this group of people didn't include volunteers for the Waffen-SS, the high command of the Wehrmacht and the General Plenipotentiary for Labour Deployment had to be briefed of this action. The OKW gave its limited consent:

> Army reserve offices are instructed to comply with the requests put forward by the *SS-* Ergänzungsstellen to carry out this action, and to clear the designated persons for the intended emergency military service, unless their service enlistment in the Wehrmacht is possible. Conscripts that are already soldiers are not eligible for clearance.

Even the General Plenipotentiary for Labour Deployment gave its approval and wrote to the President of the Regional Employment Office:

> I ask, with this kind of enlistment for long-term emergency military service, provided that no urgent functions of the war economy and food supply are affected, that no use be made of the right of objection according to the third order for securing the workforce requirements for purposes of particular national-political importance (emergency service ordinance from October 15, 1938 (RGBI I. p. 1441)).[3]

Put into practice, it went as follows:

> 1.) First, it will be verified whether the designated persons have already enlisted for military service or will be conscripted soon. In this case, nothing more will be done under notification to the SS-Hauptamt BI (4a).

> 2.) If clause 1.) does not apply, then the enlistment of the person in question will be arranged by the relevant district office, mayor, or police president of the 5th department through the emergency military service ordinance on the first day of the following month at the SS Grenadier 1st Battalion East, Breslau for the purpose of being fitted for uniforms and transfer to the Sonderkommando Dirlwanger.
> *Problems that may arise with employment offices, army reserve offices, etc., should be resolved by referring to the appropriate regulations...*

3.) If the designated persons are currently in jail or prison, then the procedure is to be returned to the office BI (4a) immediately. In this case, transfer from here to the Sonderkommando is arranged by the Reich's Criminal Police Bureau.

4.) Enlistment of this person by the Ergänzungsstelle is carried out with…the following forms: Approval by the employment office…and the Army Regional Command are to be obtained. Upon receipt of the approval of both offices, the prepared enlistment order must be transferred with a small ticket for the Waffen-SS by means of writing to the appropriate district authority, mayor, or police president (5th department) (in some cities, the mayor transfers authority for emergency service obligation to the police president) for further action.

The enlistment order and the proposal letter are to be signed by the head of the Ergänzungsstelle…

With conscripted soldiers (born after 1894), the following note should be added to the enlistment order:

You are liable to military service and therefore have to report your enlistment for long-term emergency service – likely longer than 60 days – to the appropriate Army reserve office.

Concurrent with the mailing of the enlistment order, notifying the appropriate authorities of the NSDAP in writing must take place.[4] Persons with a degree of fitness up to gvH can be enlisted; in exceptional cases, av. SS suitability and minimum size does not apply.[5]

When only around 50 men could be designated due to the strict standards – and only a fraction of these men were fit – the requirements were quickly and repeatedly reduced. The *Wilddiebkommando*, established on July 1, 1940, attained the strength of a company and was called Oranienburg, after the name of the concentration camp Sachsenhausen[6] near Oranienburg, where the *Sonderkommando* was formed.

After nearly two months of training, the *Wilddiebkommando* Oranienburg, which was renamed the *SS-Sonderkommando* Dirlewanger, was transferred to the General Government. The *Kommando* then continued training in Lublin, and was soon used to guard a Jewish work camp in Dzikow-Stary. After the war, a former member made this statement before criminal investigators:

It's true that there was a Jewish camp in Dzikow-Stary. It was under Dirlewanger's control. Some of us stood watch at the camp. I myself functioned as guard commander of the camp. It was located immediately adjacent to the rectory. It was fenced in with barbed wire. There were probably 60-100 people there. They lived within this camp in a building that could have been a barn before this... A prisoner was shot in this camp by one of our men in the late evening hours. The prisoners were singing and had been asked to quiet down by the guards, but they were unsuccessful. After that, a guard shot into the area through a knothole and accidentally killed a prisoner. The shooter was arrested, and was immediately sent to a concentration camp. That's what we were told anyway. To my knowledge, no other prisoners were shot or otherwise intentionally killed in this camp...

In spring 1941, part of the *SS-Sonderkommando* Dirlewanger went to Lemberg. There too, they guarded a Jewish work camp with around 200 Jewish men. Everywhere the *SS -Sonderkommando* was deployed in the General Government, they attracted attention with their constant plundering and murder. Then the SS and Police Court VI in Krakow initiated an investigation in the fall of 1941 which was expected to end with the imprisonment of Dirlwanger and his men. To prevent this from happening, *SS-Gruppenführer* Berger arranged for the *SS-Sonderkommando* Dirlewanger to be relocated to Belarus in January 1942.

On January 29, 1942, the *SS-Führungshauptamt* ordered the *Sonderkommando* Dirlwanger of the Waffen-SS to be placed under the control of the *Reichsführer-SS*, to take effect immediately.[7] After receiving their equipment and uniforms, they were sent to the Higher SS and Police Leader for central Russia on February 10, 1942. The *SS-Sonderkommando* was initially housed in a former old-age home in Mogilev, and eventually set up quarters in Lahoysk Palace.

This began a two-and-a-half year operation in Belarus. The Higher SS and Police Leader of central Russia, *SS-Obergruppenführer* and Police General Von dem Bach, placed the unit under control of the SS and Police Leader in Belarus, *SS-Brigadeführer* and Lieutenant-General of the Police, Kurt von Gottberg.[8]

Initially made up only of poachers, the *SS-Sonderkommando* was reinforced in May 1942 with 60 Ukrainian volunteers (former prisoners of war) due to a lack of personnel. Renamed *SS-Sonderbataillon* Dirlewanger, the unit grew in numbers with Russian volunteers and concentration camp prisoners.[9] On June 8, 1943, it had the following structure:

- German company with 150 members
- Motorcycle platoon with 40 members
- 3 Russian companies with 450 members in total
- 1 artillery battery with 40 Germans and 40 Russians

After assignment of 320 concentration camp prisoners, who weren't poachers anymore, the *SS-Sonderkommando* had already attained the following troop levels in the summer of 1943:

- Headquarters company with motorcycle platoon
- 1. (German) company
- 2. (Recruits) company (concentration camp prisoners)
- 3. (Recruits) company (concentration camp prisoners)
- 4. (Russian) company
- 5. (Russian) company

The average age of German battalion members was ca. 40 years. The average age of foreign volunteers was about 25 years. In the spring of 1944, there was an attempt to bring the *SS-Sonderbatallion* to regiment strength with more prisoner secondments from German concentration camps, but this resulted in more problems. The men first had to go through military training, which diminished the unit's deployment capacity. In addition, Dirlewanger began to lose control over the most undisciplined criminal. In order to counter this lack of authority, Dirlewanger and his proxy, Weisse, instituted draconian punishments and death sentences. Attempts to further increase the size of the unit with foreign soldiers could only be achieved partially and for a short period.

With the German retreat out of the Soviet Union, the period of occupation in Belarus by these troops, now named the *SS-Sonderregiment* Dirlewanger, also ended. Himmler reported about the unit at the Gauleiter Conference in Posen on August 1, 1944, where he knowingly made false statements. Calling these men "respectable and brave" can be traced back to the fact that he had been held responsible for the excesses of the unit by various sides of the party and the Wehrmacht.

In 1941, I set up the poacher regiment Dirlewanger. Dirlewanger is a brave Swabian, was injured ten times and is genuine. The Führer gave me permission to release all poachers from German prisons who are rifle hunters, not Kugelwilderer or snare hunters. There were roughly 2,000 of them. I'm afraid only 400 of these respectable and brave men are alive today. I have replenished this regiment again and again with probation troops from the SS – we have a terribly strict jurisdiction in the SS … After that still wasn't enough, I said to Dirlewanger, "Select some suitable candidates from our concentration camp thugs, from the career criminals." Granted, the behavior of the regiment is, I have to say, medieval in many cases, with floggings, etc. If one of them questions whether we will win the war, he'll fall dead from the table, because someone else will throw him under the bus. There's no other way to handle such people. This regiment came out of this incredible collapse with 1,200 men, including 1,000 Turkmen. They came back, marching bravely through the Russians, and only six weeks before this, they had been in a concentration camp. They were fully equipped too.

On August 1, 1944, after only a few days of rest in Lyck/East Prussia, the operation to suppress the Warsaw Uprising took place. Two months later, the SS-

Sonderregiment Dirlewanger was deployed to the battle of the Slovakian national uprising.[10] On December 16, 1944, the unit increased in size to become *SS-Sturmbrigade* Dirlewanger.[11]

Around 2,000 men, mostly political prisoners from concentration camps, were brought in to set up the second *SS-Sturmregiment*. Hundreds of them deserted to the Red Army during the first operation near Ipolysag (Hungary).

At the end of January 1945, the *SS-Sturmbrigade* Dirlewanger was ordered from Slovakia on the Oder front to the area near Guben. On February 12, 1945, they were put under command of the XXXX Panzer Corps. Some participated in the German counterattack two days later. During these battles, the *SS-Sturmbrigade* was mentioned several times in the war diary of the OKW:

> The 8th Panzer Division, in battle northeast of Luban, where the enemy has now appeared before the city. Remote battles near Nauenburg, and in the Kwisa region. More pressure near Zagan, where one of our own groups is surrounded. But we succeeded in slowing down the initial fluent strike by the enemy. The enemy pushed to the southwest near Krosno, which is why our own wing was bent back. The Dirlewanger Bridade is pushing against them from the north. On the whole, no significant change in the situation.
>
> February 1945 - Resistance in the Zagan area. The surrounded group, whose numbers have been drastically reduced, were almost able to break free. The Dirlewanger Brigade in further action to the southwest. Resistance near Guben.

On March 3, 1945, Himmler ordered the *SS-Sturmbrigade* Dirlewanger to the 36th Waffen Grenadier Division of the SS to increase troop levels. In addition to criminal and political concentration camp prisoners and delinquent Wehrmancht and SS members, regular army members joined Dirlewanger's commando. After Dirlewanger was injured in February 1945, SS *Standartenfuhrer* Schmedes assumed command. Standing on the Oder, the motley bunch experienced the Soviet attack on Berlin in April 1945. After retreating in a northwest direction with heavy losses, the rest of the division went down in Halbe, within the encircled area.

With the war's end in May 1945, the story of *SS-Sonderkommando* Dirlewanger finally came to an end after almost five years. The constantly increasing need for soldiers had led to a draft selection. Due to the age distribution of the German members, as well as the fact that the majority of the unit was made up of foreign volunteers, they were deployed to occupied Belarus. During their collection of agricultural goods from farmers and their battles with partisans, the unit acted with great ruthlessness and brutality. Even though various civilian and military agencies tried to intervene, Dirlewanger represented an executive organ of Hiltler taking aim in the east, and was able to operate unrestrained until the end.

Actual Troop Reports[12]

DATE	COMMANDERS	OFFICERS	SOLDIERS	TOTAL
1/29/1942	7	71	481	559
5/20/1943	10	71	531	612
9/11/1943	8	43	360	411
12/25/1943	5	24	172(dt.)/160(fv.)	361
2/8/1944	6	44	209(dt.)/201(fv.)	460
4/15/1944	8	38	388	434
6/1/1944	8	50	408(dt.)/241(fv.)	707
6/30/1944	17	87	867	971

Timeline of the SS-Sonderkommando Dirlewanger

The following chronology was created thanks to preserved documents. It gives an overview of the deployments of the *SS-Sonderkommando* from 1942 to 1944. A selection of orders, reports and communications appears in the appendix.

1942

3/2 – 3/10	Operation against partisans northeast of Assipowitschy.
3/12	Defense of a partisan attack on Klitschew (30 km west of Tschetschewitschi) and battles near Tscherwakow.
3/12	Pursued partisans, captured the fortified town Usochi.
3/16 – 3/22	Battle with partisans in the forests southwest of Mogilev.
3/24 – 3/28	Won over the streets of Mogilev – Bobruysk that were controlled by partisans.
4/1 – 4/5	Aided a surrounded Wehrmacht unit near Illisowa and occupied the villages Selleri and Lushiza. Pursued fleeing partisans in marshy terrain until Bazewitschi.
4/8 – 4/15	Battles near Tschetschewitschi.
4/26	Reconnaissance missions in the partisan republic Usekino.
5/3	Reconnaissance trip to Tschetschewitschi.
5/7 – 5/11	Repaired the bad roads and in the vicinity of the living quarters and restored a bridge to Mogilev.

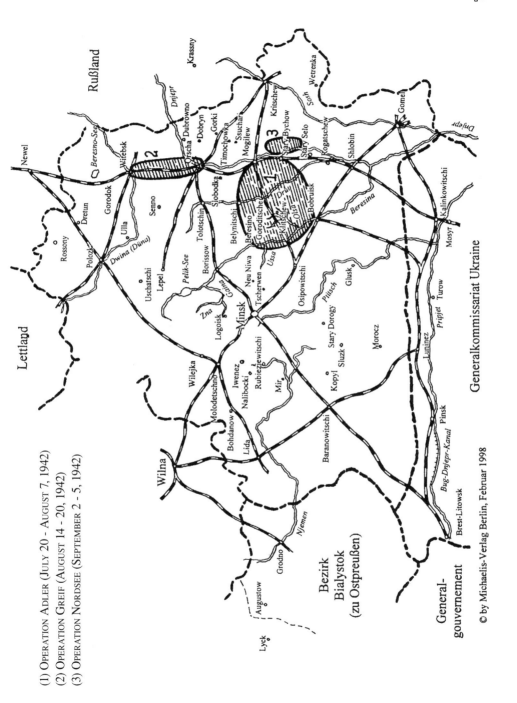

(1) Operation Adler (July 20 - August 7, 1942)
(2) Operation Greif (August 14 - 20, 1942)
(3) Operation Nordsee (September 2 - 5, 1942)

© by Michaelis-Verlag Berlin, Februar 1998

5/8 – 5/13	Mission as part of the combat group Schimana near Usekino and Sucha. Burned village of Sucha to the ground.
5/24 – 5/29	Reconnaissance and battles in the Dolgoje area.
5/25	Partisan attack on a truck belonging to the commando
5/29	Sixty volunteers of the Ukranian Schuma (auxilliary police battalion) are delegated to the commando.
5/31	Reconnaissance trips to Sbyschin, Borki, Grabowez, Chowow, Kokotowo, Chrelew and Ulolotje.
6/1	Searched the towns Stary Jusin, Gribowa Sloboda, Dolgoje, Simanowka and Alexandrowka.
6/2 – 6/5	Single operation in the forest area between Orscha and Bastocholi.
6/4 – 6/9	Deployments against partisans near Klitschew and Wojewitschi.
6/10 – 6/16	Participated in a large operation with Wehrmacht and police units in area northwest of Orscha
6/16	Action along the road from Mogilev to Rogatschew, after 17 policemen were killed by partisans
6/19	Capture of a partisan camp in the forest near Stochowtschina and recovery of a crashed German airplane in the vicinity of Wetrenka
6/21	Reconnaissance mission in wetlands northwest of Usekino
6/22	Battles with a powerful partisan group near Nowy Gorodok and repair of a bridge on the road from Mogilev to Bobruysk, 2.5km before the Gluchaja-Sseliba crossing.
6/26	Combed through the forests situated south of Saborje - Dubrowschtschina from the south (Michalewka) to the north to the top of Dijewka
6/28	Captured the heavily fortified and defended town Stary Richow and Lubianka with air support
7/3 – 7/11	Deployed with Wehrmacht members during an operation against a strong partisan group near Klitschew
7/17	Encirclement and annihilation of partisans near Titakowoitsche.
7/19	Battles near Kresnica
7/20 – 8/7	Start of Operation Adler in the triangle Mogilev - Beresino - Bobruysk - Mogilev. Deployed near Tschetschewitschi.
8/14 – 8/20	Deployment during Operation Greif west and east of the road Orscha - Witebsk.
8/23	Deployed near Usekino
8/25 – 8/28	Deployment on the road near Rogatschew

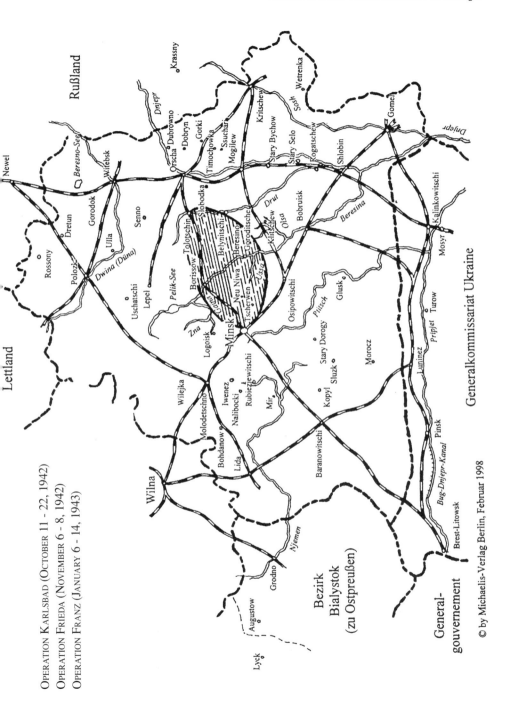

Lettland

Rußland

Newel

Beresno-See

Krassny

Dnjepr

Dubrowno
Oscha
Dobryn
Gorki
Timoczowka
Mogilew
Ssuchar
Stary Bychow
Stary Selo
Kritschew
Sosh
Wetrenka
Rogatschew
Shlobin
Gomel

Dnjepr

Kalinkowitschi
Mosyr

Witebsk

Gorodok
Dretun
Ulla
Senno
Slobodka
Tolotschin
Belynitschi
Drut
Beresino
Klitschew
Bobruisk
Olsa
Osja
Ogroditsche
Beresina

Rossony
Polozk
Dwina (Düna)
Uschatschi
Lepel
Pelik-See
Borissow
Gorod
Neu Niwa
Tscherwen
Zna
Logoisk
Osipowitschi
Glusk
Plitsch
Stary Dorogy
Sluzk
Morocz
Luninez
Pripjet
Turow

Minsk
Wilejka
Iwenez
Nalibocki
Rubiezjewitschi
Mir
Kopyl

Molodetschno
Bohdanow
Lida

Baranowitschi

Wilna

Njemen

Bug-Dnjepr-Kanal
Pinsk
Brest-Litowsk

Grodno

Augustow

Lyck

Generalkommissariat Ukraine

Bezirk
Bialystok
(zu Ostpreußen)

General-
gouvernement

© by Michaelis-Verlag Berlin, Februar 1998

OPERATION KARLSBAD (OCTOBER 11 - 22, 1942)
OPERATION FRIEDA (NOVEMBER 6 - 8, 1942)
OPERATION FRANZ (JANUARY 6 - 14, 1943)

9/2 – 9/5	Deployment during Operation Nordsee east of Staiy Bychow.
9/8	Seizure of around 1,000 land mines
9/10 – 9/14	Deployments with Police Regiment 14 in the area southeast of Mogilev near Stary Bychow - Tschetschewitschi
9/17 – 9/24	Deployed to clear the road south of Tschetschewitschi.
10/4 – 10/8	Deployment during Operation Regatta south of Gorki and Rekotka.
10/11 – 10/23	Deployment during Operation Karlsbad north of the road from Berazino to Chervyen
11/2 – 11/4	Restored peace to the area on both sides of the road from Berazino to Chervyen west of the Beresina.
11/6 – 11/8	Deployment during Operation Frieda in the areas of Retschki -Makon - Striewo - Krassnoje Lake.
11/13	Renaming the SS-Sonderkommando to SS-Sonderbataillon.
12/26	Freed the road from Berazino to Chervyen.

1943

1/2	Secured various destroyed bridges over the Ussa.
1/6 – 1/14	Deployment during Operation Franz southeast of Chervyen in the Pirunoff Most - Wesseloff - Grotsjanka – Kolejna area.
1/18 – 1/27	Deployment and acquisition of agricultural goods during Operation Erntefest I in the area northeast of Sluzk.
1/29	Commando introduces its own collar patch. Instead of SS runes, the men now carry two crossed rifles under which a stick hand grenade lays horizontally.
1/30 – 2/15	Deployment during Operation Erntefest II in the area of Minsk - Iwenez up to the Sluzk – Brest road.
2/2	Seveny-eight Russians are shot in Sadkowazczyzna and 18 farms are burned down. Around 110 heads of livestock are handed over to the District Agricultural Leader.
2/3	Eleven partisans and 43 relatives are shot.
2/16 – 2/26	Deployment during Operation Hornung in the Pripyat Marshes (in the Morocz – Milewicze area) against partisans, who have interrupted traffic on the rail line Gomel - Luninez - Brest. Simultaneous acquisition of agricultural commodities. Local drivers of the sled columns are

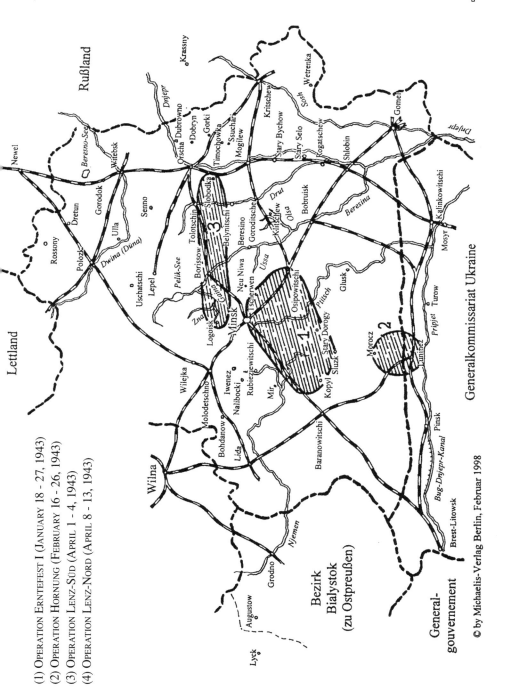

(1) Operation Erntefest I (January 18 - 27, 1943)
(2) Operation Hornung (February 16 - 26, 1943)
(3) Operation Lenz-Süd (April 1 - 4, 1943)
(4) Operation Lenz-Nord (April 8 - 13, 1943)

© by Michaelis-Verlag Berlin, Februar 1998

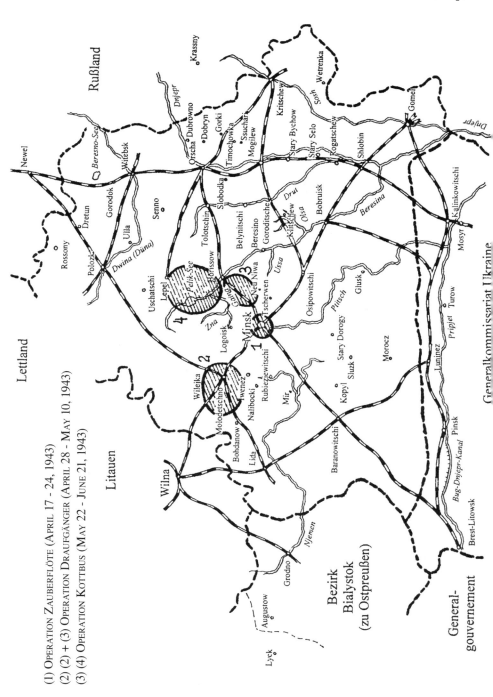

(1) Operation Zauberflöte (April 17 - 24, 1943)
(2) (2) + (3) Operation Draufgänger (April 28 - May 10, 1943)
(3) (4) Operation Kottbus (May 22 - June 21, 1943)

ordered to remain behind when villages are destroyed so that they are not present during mass shootings. In total, 1,272 dead partisans, 1,211 murdered civilians and 104 prisoners are counted.

2/26	Guidelines for partisan warfare are published by representatives of the Reichsführer-SS, SS-Obergruppenführer Von dem Bach.
2/27 – 4/16	Local action in the area around the living quarters in Lahoysk.
4/1 – 4/4	Deployment during Operation Lenz-Süd in the marshy forest area south of the Borissow - Slobodka – Smolewitsche area.
4/8 – 4/13	Deployment during Operation Lenz-Nord in the Borissow - Smolewitsche - Lahoysk - Sembin area.
4/17 – 4/24	Deployment during Operation Zauberflöte in the Belarusian capital Minsk. The Jewish Ghetto is cordoned off.
4/28 – 5/10	Deployment during Operation Draufgänger I and II in the Molodetschno and Manila – Rudnja-Wald areas.
5/4	Suspected partisand village Brygidowa is destroyed. Around 60 men, women and children are killed. During this action, a total of 386 partisans and 294 suspected partisans are shot. Starzynki, Brygidowo, Lubca, Batuiyn, Krzeminiec und Januszkowicze are some of the villages that are burned to the ground.
5/11 – 5/12	Securing the Sloboda area.
5/22 – 6/21	Deployment during Operation Kottbus to suppress the partisan republic in the Pelik Lake area. Civilians are driven from the heavily-mined area. German losses total about 120 dead and 1,000 wounded, almost 5,000 men and over 1,000 women are listed for the transport to Germany. Over 10,000 partisans and civilians also died. Almost 1,000 were taken prisoner.
6/29 – 7/7	Deployment in Operation Günther in the Manila – Rudnja-Wald area.
7/7 – 8/5	Deployment during Operation Hermann in the Nalibocki-Wald area(Mir - Rubieziewitschi - Rakow - Cholchlo - Bohdanow).
7/21	A partisan and 287 suspected partisans are shot near Plopki. Dubowce and its inhabitants are burned down.
8/1	Large evacuation effort as part of Operation Hermann in the Jeremicze - Starzyna - Rudnja – Kupisk area.
11/1 – 11/4	Deployment during Operation Heinrich to crush the partisan republic Rossony in the Polotsk - Krassnopolje - Pustoschka - Idriza - Sebesh area.
11/5	Defensive trench warfare battles in the areas north and northeast of Polotsk (Beresno-Lake). Put under the command of a Latvian SS company.[55]

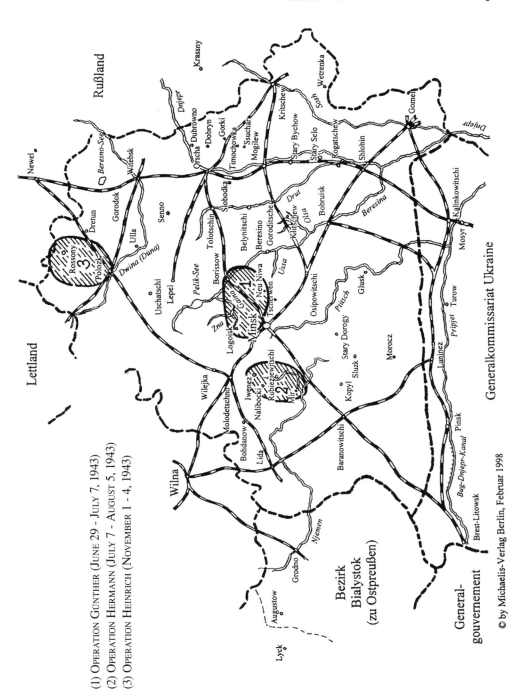

(1) Operation Günther (June 29 - July 7, 1943)
(2) Operation Hermann (July 7 - August 5, 1943)
(3) Operation Heinrich (November 1 - 4, 1943)

© by Michaelis-Verlag Berlin, Februar 1998

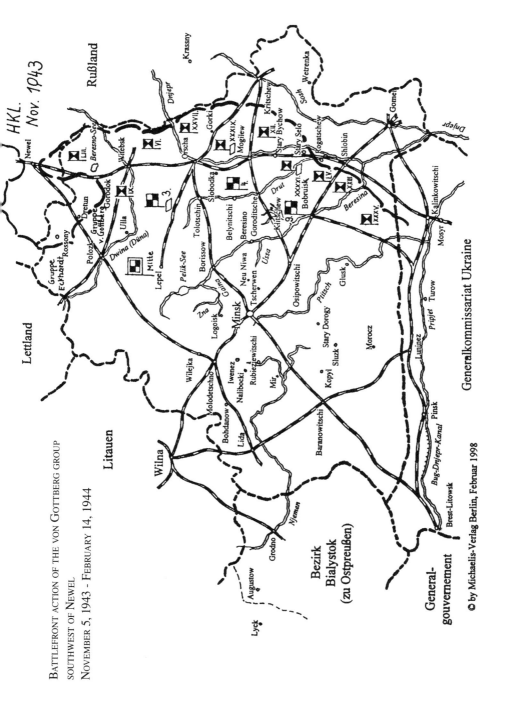

BATTLEFRONT ACTION OF THE VON GOTTBERG GROUP
SOUTHWEST OF NEWEL
NOVEMBER 5, 1943 - FEBRUARY 14, 1944

1944

1/10	Command of the battalion by SS-Hauptsturmführer Weisse (1. combat group "Mißmahl"11 and 2. combat group "Licis").
2/15	End of front lines deployment south of Newel. March back to Lohoisk.
4/2	Safeguarding a food convoy to Nisok.
4/16–5/12	Deployment during Operation Frühlingsfest in the greater Uschatschi area.
5/00	The SS-Sonderbataillon is renamed an SS-Sonderregiment
6/22	Start of the Soviet summer offensive.[56] Deployment as part of the combat group von Gottberg in the Nalibocki-Wald area.
7/7	After the Soviet advance on Lida, occupation of a fortified position and attack of the flanks of the enemy. Successful counter strike by the enemy forcing German troops on the road to East Prussia.
7/29	After heavy retreat battles in the Grodno - Augustow area, the rest reach the military training complex in Lyck and are replenished here.[57]

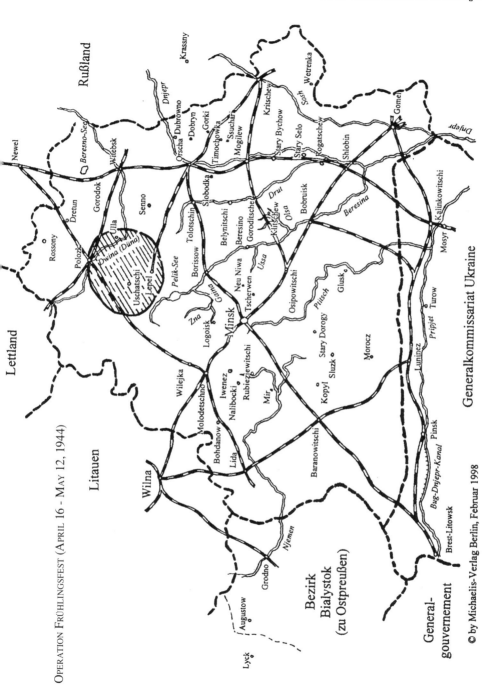

OPERATION FRÜHLINGSFEST (APRIL 16 - MAY 12, 1944)

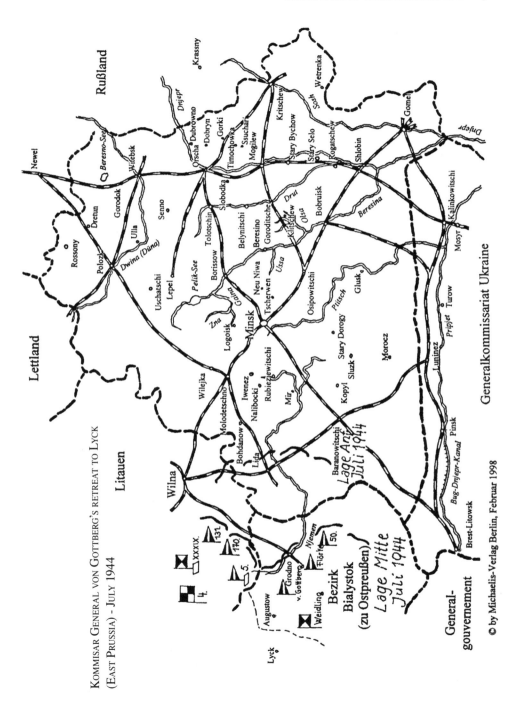

KOMMISAR GENERAL VON GOTTBERG'S RETREAT TO LYCK
(EAST PRUSSIA) - JULY 1944

© by Michaelis-Verlag Berlin, Februar 1998

Endnotes

1   Gottlieb Berger was born on July 16, 1896, in Gerstetten (Württemberg). He joined the NSDAP, and in 1932 he led the *SA-Untergruppe Württemberg*. With the rank of *SS-Oberführer*, he was accepted into the SS on January 30, 1936. On April 20, 1939, he obtained the rank of *SS-Brigadeführer* and became the head of the Replenishment Office. Two years later, promotion to *SS-Gruppenführer* and the appointment as head of the SS-Main Office followed. On June 21, 1943, he was promoted to *SS-Obergruppenführer* and General of the Waffen-SS. In addition to numerous state positions (in the Ostministerium, among others), he was also a district professional hunter. Thus, there was also a connection to the poachers here.

2   King Heinrich I was born in 875 A.D., and was King of Germany from 919 until his death in 936. He defeated the Slavs in 928/29 and conquered Brandenburg. In 933, he defeated the invading Hungarians on the Unstrut.

3   This probation allowed for "a firm membership of 2 years to the *SS-Sonderkommando* and a decoration for bravery awarded, where applicable."

4   *garnisonsverwendungsfähig* (garrison usable homeland)

5   *arbeitsverwendungsfähig* (usable for work)

6   The concentration camp was a collection camp for replacements until the fall of 1944. In the beginning, the unit was also managed within the *5ᵗʰ Totenkopf Unit Oranienburg*, until they were eventually incorporated themselves.

7   With regard to the Russian campaign, an emergency committee of the *Reichsführer-SS* was formed on Himmler's command on April 7, 1941. Renamed the *Reichsführer-SS* headquarters on May 6, 1941, it succeeded in attacking the Soviet Union in the already occupied territories and performed special operations that resulted from the war of ideologies. Tens of thousands of civilians died in this ethnic cleansing.

8   Kurt von Gottberg was born on February 11, 1896, in Wilten, Prussia. He participated in the First World War and was awarded Iron Crosses, 1st and 2nd Class. Discharged as First Lieutenant, he was a member of the Ehrard Brigade from 1919 to 1924. In 1932 he joined the NSDAP, as well as the SS (SS-Nr. 45.923), and worked from 1937 to 1939 in the Rasse und Siedlungshauptamt (Race and Settlement Main Office). As SS-Oberführer he led the Bodenamt (Land Office) in Prague. From October 1, 1940, to July 21, 1942, he was chief of the Erfassungsamt (Acquisition Office) in the SS-Hauptamt. With the promotion to SS-Brigadeführer and General Major of the Police, he took over the office of SS and Police Leader of Belarus, and on March 24, 1943, he was appointed as a representative of the Higher SS and Police Leader of central Russia. On July 15, 1943, his appointment to SS-Gruppenführer and Lieutenant-General of the Police followed. Nine days after eventually taking over the office of the Higher SS and Police Leader of central Russia on June 21, 1944, he was promoted to SS-Obergruppenführer and General of the Waffen-SS and Police. On July 20, 1944, he

was awarded the Knight's Cross of the Iron Cross. After he was captured by the Allies, he committed suicide in Flensburg on May 31, 1945.

9   Volunteers

10   cf. Michaelis, Rolf. *Der Weg zur 36.Waffen-Grenadier-Division der SS, Rodgau 1991 und ders.: Die Grenadier-Divisionen der Waffen-SS (Teil III).* Erlangen, 1995.

11   SS-FHA Tgb.Nr. 4897/44 geh.Kdos. Dr. Buno Wille gave the following graphic information about the circumstances regarding the *SS-Sturmbrigade* on June 28, 1946:
I was the 2nd judge at the field court of the *SS Panzergrenadier* Division in November 1944, when I received the transfer decree for the *Sturmbrigade* Dirlewanger from my supervising office, the SS Court Head Office. Before that, I had only known about the unit by hearsay as the poacher's-probation battalion...
I was told by *Standartenführer* Burmeister, the head of the Clemency Department, that penalized SS-probation troops were also with the *Sturmbrigade* in a limited scope by express command of Himmler, and that I would be sent there to regulate the rehabilitation cases for these troops, since cooperation between the SS Court Head Office and Dirlwanger couldn't be achieved in this regard.
I found out from the chief of the Head Office, *SS Obergruppenführer* Breithaupt, that an SS-court, to which I could have come as an SS-judge, did not exist in the *Sturmbrigade*, and that the nearest SS and Police court was responsible for newly delinquent SS members and previous SS members, while the commander, *SS Oberführer* Dirlewanger, had the unlimited right over life and death of all other members of the brigade, which was due to an order from the *Reichsführer-SS* and happened to be "top secret"...
In early December 1944, I met up with the brigade in Slovakia. The conditions that I found there were such that I couldn't justify a slow, careful approach, in the interest of humanity and justice... Neither the composition, nor the command of this unit resembled an SS-unit, apart from the fact that they were at least wearing SS uniforms. From various statements by Dirlwanger and observing the practice during the short time of my presence, I believe I am able to say that the central command of the entire Waffen-SS, the *SS-Führungshauptamt*, had no power or authority over the *Sturmbrigade*, but rather that Dirlwanger's questions directly involving Himmler, with whom he enjoyed a preferred position, were managed by *SS-Obergruppenführer* Nebe from the *Reichskriminalpolizeiamt* or his intimate friend, *SS-Obergruppenführer* Berger, who did everything for him.
Inquiries and complaints from other offices, head offices among them, were simply thrown into the wastebasket if they were unpleasant, and Dirlewanger always invoked his position with Himmler. The administration of justice in the brigade was shocking. Reports to an SS and Police Court were never turned in. Dirlewanger just took care of everything himself, further exceeding his authorization over life and death, no matter whether it involved still innocent or already punished, concentration camp prisoners, or Wehrmacht or former SS members. Punishment included only beatings or the death penalty, as the command of the entire unit was built on beatings...
O*n the third day of my presence, when I had appropriate insight, I already pointed out the unsustainable conditions to Dirlewanger and proposed suitable changes to him...*
When I further insisted and emphasized that what was happening in the brigade was flat-out murder, and with reference to my oath as judge, that I rejected even the smallest actions under these conditions, he broke me off so that I was unable to have any more influence whatsoever. Because I didn't dare to do it from the brigade, I gave, at the first opportunity, on the occasion of an official trip to the SS and Police Court in Pressburg, a truthful report about the abuses of the brigade...
I was then transferred to another unit, partly due to the expected ill will from Dirlewanger through my actions, which excluded a fruitful collaboration from the start in terms of jurisdiction, and partly due to my personal safety...

12   Where the following report doesn't disclose, total troop numbers are composed of around 50% Germans (dt.) and 50% foreign volunteers (fv.), mainly Russians and Ukrainians.

55   In early October 1943, the Red Army surprisingly broke through in a what had been a quiet section of a Luftwaffen field division east of Newel on the border between the army groups Nord and Mitte (lö.Armee und 3.PzArmee) and seized the Newel communications junction. Combat groups were quickly formed, which were to halt the enemy's advance. At the same time, the Army group Nord asked Wehrmacht commander in Ostland (Cavalry General Braemer) to secure the nearby Latvian border. On October 12th the Gren.Rgt. 374 began a counterattack north of the Polotsk – Newel rail line. In early November, further reinforcements arrived at the front. In addition to the 290th and 122nd Infantry Divisions, the SS-Sonderbataillon was also deployed to the front. Despite heavy German resistance, the enemy managed to block the Pustoschka – Newel road on November 8, 1943. An attempt by the 23rd and 32nd Infantry Divisions to advance from the Pustoschka – Newel road west to Jasno Lake ran aground. At the end of 1943, the order came to evacuate the section. All attempts to close up the huge point of incursion failed. To avert the danger of German troops being encircled on the front lines jutting out south from Pustoschka to Newel, relocation began on New Year's Day.

56   Within the first few days, the Soviet troops were already able to penetrate deep into the retreating Army's territory. On July 2nd, the Red Army blocked the Minsk – Molodecno road. Other troops, coming from Bobruisk, eventually stood southeast of Minsk. When Soviet tanks advanced from the north via Lohoisk to the Belarusian capital, members of the 4th Army, who were still retreating via Beresina, got through the enclosure southeast of Minsk. On July 3, 1944, Soviet troops from the 3rd Army moved into Minsk. In total, there were 28 German divisions inside the enclosure east of Minsk with about 350,000 soldiers. All but a few, who were able to fight back to the west, ended up prisoners of war or were killed. Wilna (Orders Command 3rd Panzer Army), which formed the seam between the 3rd Panzer Army and the 4th Army, was supposed to be in a firm position to become a focal point for the German defense. The left flank of the 4th Army set up in an area west of Minsk – Wilna the XXXIX.PzK (131., 170.ID). In a southern direction, the Corps group Weidling (5.PD, KGr. "von Gottberg," KGr. "Flörke," 50.ID) joined them.

57   Between the 3rd Panzer Army [right flank: XXXIX.AK] and the 4th Army [left flank: VI.AK (Weidling group) consisting of KGr von Gottberg, 50.ID, 14.ID and 3.SS-PD] there was a gaping hole of around 30 km. The Red Army was able to overrun the left flank of the 4th Army on both sides of the Wasiliszki and throw them back to Ostryna. The Soviet Cavalry stood on the Grodno - Wilna railway line. The VI.AK then retreated back behind the Njemen. The KGr von Gottberg formed an eastern bridgehead near Grodno, over the Njemen. Members of the combat group began to march in a northern direction in order to halt the Soviet advance, which only succeeded temporarily. On July 14th, enemy troops tried to penetrate the bridgehead from the north and south near Grodno. On July 18th, the enemy units stood farther north on the Seenge in Augustowo. To close the 30 km gap on the front, the 3rd SS Panzer Division Totenkopf was ordered from Grodno toward Augustowo. The 5th PD came from the north. The combat group von Gottberg received the order to support the forward march of the SS-Division Totenkopf. The attack closed the gap on the front, and the line of defense was stabilized. On July 24th, the Red Army troops were able to break in 50 km south of Grodno in Sokolka. Between the eastern edge of town and the 12th PD two km to the west, a new gap in the front was created. Together with a combat group from the 3rd Panzer Division, the combat group von Gottberg was engaged in a limited counterattack on Sokolka - Kuznica - Karolin – Lipsk. This gap couldn't be closed either. The 3rd Panzer Division began to march the following day to AOK 2 in Siedlice (80 km east of Warsaw), and the combat group von Gottberg took over command of the right flank as Generalkommando von Gottberg. The Weidling group took over the left Army flank in the Augustowo area.

Bibliography

Michaelis, Rolf. *Das SS-Sonderkommando "Dirlewanger"*, Berlin 1998
Michaelis, Rolf. *Die SS-Sturmbrigade "Dirlewanger"*, Berlin 2003

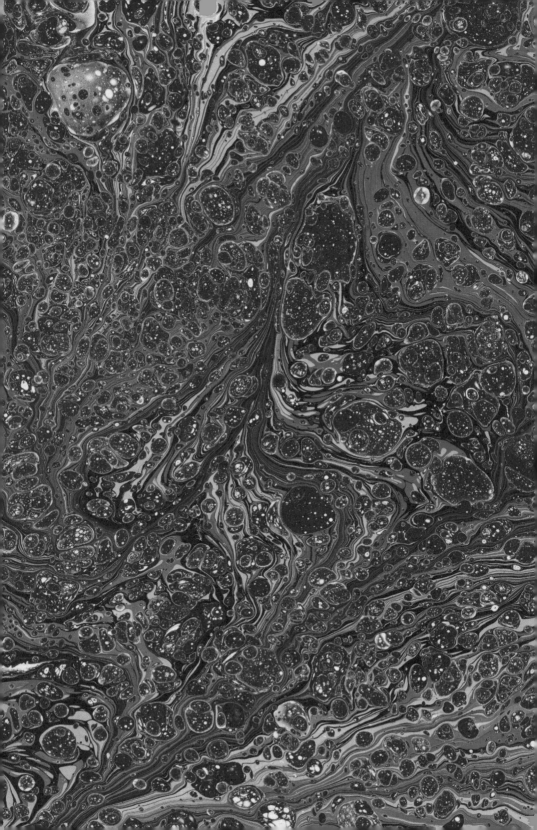